MW01242668

ADVERSA FACIT VICTORIAM SUAVIUS.
Latin for: "Adversity Makes the Victory Sweeter."

Advance Praise

DISRUPTED! is a pointed yet compassionate look at stress that takes you under the hood, so to speak, in straight forward language, and shows you how to develop coping skills to not only survive but thrive. Dr. Makai understands that life is not measured by what you accomplish, but by what you overcome in order to accomplish it. If you're looking for something quick, yet deep, to the point that it is a quick read that can support you in better coping with stress and disruption, read DISRUPTED!

Steve Scott, the Houston Business Coach and author of "Wings to Fly"

This concise and content-rich book highlights disruption and the value it can bring to our lives. Dr. Makai illustrates disruption as something to run toward and embrace with excitement, rather than something to shy away from fearfully. With each chapter, he shows us that resiliency can be learned and provides valuable, ready-to-use "toolbox" items that can be applied in many areas of life.

In DISRUPTED!, Dr. Makai helps us see that it's a personal choice to accept and react accordingly to obstacles – good and bad – that show up in our life and our responsibility to adapt and overcome, as needed. He reminds us that we have the choice to either live in the past, dwell on the present, or to move forward with excitement to live our best lives and to make a difference in the lives of others.

Barbara Griffin, Corporate Learning & Development Professional

DISRUPTED!

RESILIENTLY REINTEGRATING AFTER STRESS & ADVERSITY

**Other Books
by
Dr. Kozhi Sidney Makai**

How Can I Come Up?

Born Beating the Odds™

Puzzle Pieces

Culture & Leadership

Our 'I Dos' Were...Different

Communication Training & Development

DISRUPTED!

RESILIENTLY REINTEGRATING AFTER STRESS & ADVERSITY

Kozhi Sidney Makai, Ph.D, Psy.D

© 2020 Kozhi Sidney Makai, Ph.D, Psy.D. All rights reserved. No part of this publication may be reproduced, stored in a retrieval system, or transmitted by any means – electronic, mechanical, photocopy, recording, or any other – except for brief quotations in reviews, without the prior permission of the author.

This book is a work of non-fiction. Unless otherwise noted, the author and the publisher make no explicit guarantees as to the accuracy of the information contained in this book and, in some cases, names of people and places have been altered to protect their privacy.

ISBN: 978-0-9799891-2-4

Cover design by adWhite (www.adWhite.com)

Printed in the United States of America

SPECIAL SALES

Scrolls & Scribes Books are available at special discounts for bulk purchases for sales promotions or premiums. Special editions, including personalized covers, excerpts of existing books, and corporate imprints, can be created in large quantities for special needs. For information, email SpecialMarkets@KozhiMakai.com

Acknowledgments

*FEW DISCOVERIES TAKE PLACE IN A VACUUM. WHILE MANY PEOPLE
MIGHT LIKE TO TAKE FULL CREDIT FOR THEIR NEW VISIONS, THE
FACT IS WE ARE ALWAYS INDEBTED TO THE PAST, TO THOSE
THINKERS WHO HAVE SET THE STAGE FOR WHATEVER IT MAY BE
THAT WE HAVE COME UPON.*
Dr. Frederic Flach

Acknowledgements remain the most difficult part of my work as an author. How do you say thank you in a *meaningful* way when you have a legion of faithful and available people who never stop reminding you how proud they are of you, how much they believe in you, and how much you mean to them? Most definitely not an easy task. That in mind, thank you to my wonderful support system; you know who you are, and you make deposits in my life so often, it'll take eternity for your account with me to ever be overdrawn.

I thank God for entrusting me with this writing gift. It's brought me immense joy and has been cathartic. My Rock and Lighthouse is what Jesus is. Every challenge has been manageable because I can count on His wisdom and guidance. Every joy has been multiplied because He's enthralled by my joy. All that I am is because of Him, and my goal remains to be a *Faithful* Child of God.

Thank you, Bee, for your loyalty, love, and support. You're my best friend and my wife; writing the narrative of my life with conviction, passion, and clarity is so much easier with you by my side — I can't thank you enough for all the times we've laughed, cried, and grown from every disruption.

I get to work with one of my best friends every day. There since the beginning, and there to the end, you're indispensable Lela. Your loyalty and attention to detail makes my daily life look simple. Best friend. Executive Assistant. Chief of Staff. You wear so many hats and make it look easy.

Gabriela, mi hija, thank you for holding me to the fire every day. You've taken the role of Managing Director of

Digital Learning & Communications and run with it like you stole something! Your excellence and tireless energy bring amazing value to me personally and to our clients. Thank you for believing in me.

Glenn and Darnell: You're in my ear every day. Checking in on me and making sure I'm well and my needs are met. You guys hold me accountable with patience and love; thank you for being my wingmen for so many years.

Lauren Renee: You're the best goddaughter in the world; thank you for teaching me how to parent and allowing me to be your goddad.

To my parents, Edna, A.A.M, Renée, George, Leon, Ger, and Elesa: thank you for constantly supporting me, believing in me, and desiring the best for me. Words can't do justice to the depth of gratitude I feel for the guidance you've provided over the years.

I'd like to make a special shoutout to my 7-year old favorite friend, Elliana. Knowing that I have you across the street to always run down the driveway into my arms is special. You always remind me that I'm the best Kozhi ever and you'll love me forever — that's heartwarming and a fantastic treat, especially during disruption.

Finally, I'd like to thank Scot Pollock — my friend and my pastor. A brilliant mind and wonderful teacher, I've been blessed by your wisdom and training. Thank you for keeping it real and taking me as I am while challenging me to be and do more.

Contents

Foreword

Leadership matters. I believe this is fact. A surprising number of outcomes in your life, no matter your calling or chosen profession, will hang on leadership. Perhaps you are a leader. That may be why you picked up this book.

I'm a leader. And as a leader, I have experienced significant, complex, and diverse challenges. You have as well. Perhaps that means we're doing at least a few things right. Leaders are called into the fray. In fact, without some challenge, some problem, some vision, some goal, leaders aren't really necessary. Think about it. Leaders exist to mobilize, equip, and align others to solve, to conquer, to win.

Leadership requires challenges and tests. And these challenges, in turn, can make or break the leader. In brief, that's what *Disrupted!* is all about; the development of resiliency and the acquisition of a confident road map to navigate the disruptions that are common in life and leadership.

I'm also a pastor of a local church. As such, I'm called to operate in several realms of organizational, relational, and spiritual leadership. Interacting with a large and diverse group of people within these realms is a recipe for lots of disruption. And with more than 1,500 Christian pastors permanently leaving their jobs every month in America, believe me, these disruptions can be dramatic and life-altering.

Within the pages of the book you hold, you'll be taken on two concurrent journeys. The first journey is through intentional layers of accessible research, challenging definitions, and relevant applications. But this path is not the only story. It'll serve you in your second simultaneous journey, the one to a better you. These journeys are not mutually exclusive and won't be merely academic. They'll work together to equip you with new insight, help you renovate your personal narrative, and boost your ability to thrive in every sphere. If you're a leader, these journeys will prove invaluable.

I wish you could personally meet my friend Dr. Kozhi Sidney Makai. If you did, you would engage the living embodiment of the attitudes and actions in this book. An imposing yet welcoming stature with a wide, heartfelt smile, Kozhi would make you feel like an old friend in a matter of moments. He has spent his professional career helping people thrive. I believe you are about to find out just how exceptional he is at expressing this passion. And right now, it's aimed right at you.

Scot Pollok
Lead Pastor
Faith Bible Church

Dedication

To Tabitha Pistole Makai:
My Best Friend.
Your story is punctuated by resiliency,
and it's my pleasure to share in it every day.
I love you t-rex much.

Preface

IF YOU FAINT IN THE DAY OF ADVERSITY,
YOUR STRENGTH IS SMALL.
Proverbs 24:10

My journey towards performance psychology has been scenic. Before finally settling on performance psychology, I fell in love with the psychology of *success*. This love affair began when I arrived in New York City for the first time on February 14, 1997 — Valentine's Day. Flying into New York and seeing Lady Liberty for the first time, I was certain my life would never be the same. *Land of the Free. Home of the Brave. The Land of Opportunity.* All waiting for me to touch down and lay claim to it all. Interestingly, that was nowhere near how my story in the United States would begin...

You see, unlike Zambia, you couldn't simply buy a ticket at the airport for same day travel — especially on Valentine's Day — without incurring major price gouging. So, I chose the next best thing: a grueling, pre-WiFi *Greyhound* bus ride from New York City to Houston, Texas. Now, unless you've experienced a Greyhound bus for that many miles, you have no idea how dumb that was! In Zambia, when you get on a coach (that's what we call large buses) from, say, Lusaka to Johannesburg, South Africa, you use the same bus; as you hit major cities, passengers leave, others join, but you use the same bus. Not so with *Greyhound*; we made stops at major cities alright — and changed buses every, single time! That was the longest bus ride I've ever been on, and I'm glad to say it was the last. Though I learned a great deal about the United States from fellow passengers, what I learned most was that my dream was going to cost me much more than I had bargained for.

Resiliency is simply *impossible* without resistance, challenge, change, and disruption. If there's anything I've discovered in the years since that "fun" ride down the eastern seaboard and across the southeastern and southern United States, it's that the secret to success isn't education, connections, intelligence, or wit; the secret to success is *endurance*. As you'll learn in this tiny book, stamina, perseverance, or any other words you use for endurance, never quitting represents the difference between achievement and failure to launch. Perhaps that's why H. Jackson Brown Jr. holds the trophy to my favorite quote: *In the confrontation between the stream and the rock, the stream always wins, not through strength but by perseverance.*

My American dad, George Eberly, has been telling me for 20 years that we go into life with an empty toolbox. Along the way, we experience things — good and bad, large and small, and so on. He continues to remind me that we should take with us what we might need for the future. My dad says *we can't meet tomorrow's challenge if our toolbox is empty.* And the only way our toolbox can be empty is if we *refuse* to learn from *every* experience.

Though this little book is research-based (and I promise not to bore you with endless research notes), it's meant to remind you to *be* the stream and to *fill* your toolbox; it's meant to provide you with practical tools for taking the disruption that's common to mankind and blending it into the smoothie of a life *well-lived*. Whether you hope to succeed at home, at work, at school, or anywhere else, obstacles such as disappointments will grace the landscape; my hope is to provide you with the glasses to see how those mountains you're calling obstacles can actually beautify the painting of your life — if you'll let them.

Kozhi Sidney Makai, Ph.D, Psy.D
The Woodlands, Texas

Introduction

GREATNESS FEARS NO CONSEQUENCE.
Doug Collins

M y professional focus for the last 20 years has been using behavioral science to help people *thrive* — especially in the workplace. Because I can't reach every home in the world, I've devoted my life to the *discovery* and *delivery* of tools that make thriving accessible, possible, and easier. If I can reach people at work and teach them how to use thriving tools in *every* arena of their lives, I've played a role in helping them thrive at work, at home, and everywhere in between.

Since the days of my twenty-something-hour bus ride from New York City to Houston, Texas, I've endured hardships, distractions, heartbreaks, and pain; I've also seen others — some close to me, some not — endure similar challenges. I've learned that what was common between me and others enduring difficult times is that we ended up thriving in spite of the hardships. We were blissfully ignorant of the fact that making lemonade out of the lemons in our lives wasn't normal. Much like a bumblebee, which is *not* supposed to fly because its wingspan and body size are in the wrong proportion, we thought jumping off the ledge and flapping our wings *is* what you did after you got beaten down. As it turns out, after disappointment, not everyone gets back on the ledge or ever flaps their wings again...

I began my career on the motivational speaking circuit. I was inspired by the late Zig Ziglar and was sure that my calling in life was to motivate and inspire people into action. What began as a speaking career has now evolved into a performance improvement consulting practice that uses positive psychology principles to help clients go from Potential to Performance™. Today, it all looks like a perfectly laid out plan that worked perfectly; the reality is that there are many mistakes, missteps, and disappointments in the foundation of Kozhi Makai Worldwide. These disruptions are the iron and concrete we've used to overcome, adapt, and improvise; they are the steel that our team placed in the construction to ensure our consulting practice (we prefer to call it an idea studio) lives out its purpose every day.

Much of our work at Kozhi Makai Worldwide is done in the organizational setting. Organizations, however, don't exhibit resiliency; *people* do. Organizations are a grouping of people attempting to row in the same direction as they traverse treacherous seas while serving their stakeholders. The premises in this book are not meant to develop resiliency in organizations, per se; they are meant to spur individuals towards resiliency. As you'll discover in the chapters that follow, much of resiliency is a *choice*; while there are legitimate exceptions, you and I get to choose the path we take at the disruption fork. I'll show you what each option at the fork brings, and hope that you'll choose life — that is, thriving instead of surviving and taking ownership for your narrative instead of being a victim of life's seeming randomness.

3 Tools for Your Toolbox

1. My hardships will not stop me from flying.
2. My failures will be my steppingstones.
3. Resiliency is my daily choice

PART I

I can't stand clichés, or other things people say that are simply not true or realistic. *The best things in life are free. Do something you love, and you'll never work a day in your life. What you don't know won't hurt you.* This last one drives me nuts because what we don't know can *kill* us! Some people think the truth will set them free, but the thought begins with: You shall know the truth. It's not the truth that sets us free; it's the *knowledge* of the truth that sets us free.

In this section, I share knowledge surrounding adversity, disruption, endurance, stress, and other foundational thoughts that we need to develop resiliency. While I've done my best to be impartial, you'll quickly sense my bias towards action. Knowing the truth is wonderful; *acting* on it makes all the difference.

I'd like to point you towards actions that can make the development of resiliency simpler. I'd like to walk you through a deeper understanding of what it takes to *consistently* collect protective factors against stress and disruption. If you come at it with an open mind, I believe we can collaboratively map out a strategy that'll work for you and turn the tide so that disruption becomes a welcome sight rather than a plague to avoid.

1. Endurance

*LET US NOT LOSE HEART AND GROW WEARY AND FAINT IN ACTING
NOBLY AND DOING RIGHT, FOR IN DUE TIME AND AT THE
APPOINTED SEASON WE SHALL REAP, IF WE DO NOT LOOSEN AND
RELAX OUR COURAGE AND FAINT.*
The Apostle Paul

I enjoy running. I enjoy it and do it so often that I'm frequently asked, "Are you training for something? A marathon?" My answer is always the same: I laugh and respond that my body was not made for marathons. The longest run I've ever done is 10.05 miles. On March 24, 2010, at 9:31am, I set off on a 99-minute test of endurance. I can't say who won that day, but I can say that, as much as I love running, endurance running is not for me. A half-marathon (13.1 miles) or full (26.2 miles) just doesn't spark feelings of joy or excitement in me. Some days I envy those who do endurance sports; other days, I think they have too much time on their hands. Whatever my feelings about endurance running, life is an endurance sport; it's certainly a marathon and requires us to sometimes "hunker down" as we say down here in Texas.

Every runner is going to hit their wall. This is the point at which they haven't the energy to run anymore; the point at which the pain is so steep, their body is wailing at them to stop. So it goes with the marathon called life: We *will* hit points in life when we'll have two choices: endure or quit. While we'd all like to think that, when that moment comes, we'll stand tall and endure, we need to be honest with ourselves. All we have to do is look around us and we'll see how easy and comfortable quitting is.

The pressures and stresses of life tend to hit us on every front: we're pressured at work to perform, we're pressured at home to provide, and we're now pressured — more than ever — in the media to conform. Socially, spiritually, emotionally, financially, and professionally, we're expected to hit high marks; social media doesn't sleep, and reminds us daily about what we're not, what we don't have, or what we've lost. With all these pressures, it's very easy to quit; it's very easy to give up and simply not endure.

As you'll learn in this book, nothing great comes to a person, a community, or a culture that refuses to endure. All of life's greatest and most precious things are the result of endurance. If you can't accept that fact, I respectfully ask you to stop reading and get a refund; this book is not for you. If, however, you can accept that endurance is the key that unlocks the widest and deepest of your potential, we can work together to formulate an action-plan that'll help you use the strains, stresses, and pressures of life to live out your greatest potential. I can't guarantee that you'll be promoted, get the job, raise perfect children (if those even exist), or snag a perfect mate; what I can guarantee is that you'll look challenge in the eye and become better at refusing to be afraid or quit.

3 Tools for Your Toolbox

1. The harvest is a result of patient endurance.
2. I always have the option to quit...or to endure.
3. My potential lies just beyond enduring stress and pressure.

2. Stress

HARDSHIPS OFTEN PREPARE ORDINARY PEOPLE FOR AN
EXTRAORDINARY DESTINY.
C.S Lewis

Reknowned sports psychologist Dr. James Loehr has spent much of his career helping performers deepen their capacity for responding to stress through a vehicle he calls Toughness Training©. By toughness, Dr. Loehr doesn't mean brute force; he means a relaxed, highly focused performance energy called the *Ideal Performance State*[1]. To get performers to this point, stress must be reframed in the minds of performers because the following myths pervade our view of stress:

1. Stress is bad and should be avoided whenever possible.
2. Freedom from stress will bring you great happiness.
3. Stress undermines your health.
4. The less stress in your life, the more productive you are.
5. If you can't handle the stress, get out of the fast lane!
6. Stress capacity is inborn.
7. The greater the stress in life, the less happy you are likely to be.
8. Stressing your body and brain eventually wears them out.
9. The older you get, the more you need to protect yourself from stress.
10. The level of stress in your life is a direct reflection of how many bad things have happened to you[2].

Be honest: have you subscribed to one or more of these myths? If so, you're certainly not alone. Most of these myths come from a poor understanding of stress and, if I can be so blunt, intellectual laziness. If we were to truly engage in critical thinking around stress, we would discover that each of the myths can be debunked with both proven science and personal experience. That's why any discussion on resiliency must begin with an honest assessment of stress — both its *impact* on our health and its *power* to transform our lives.

Stress is on almost everyone's mind. We stress about our children, our commute, our retirement, the prom, our grades, our job, and even stress about stress. Research has found that stress can have serious implications for our general health and welfare, including our mental health and performance[3]. Because of the negative connotations attached to the word stress, as evidenced by what you've just read, it's important that we define stress and then distinguish between *good* stress and *bad* stress.

Stress is the *payment* we must all make as part of human existence[4]. We can't create a *meaningful* life or accomplish *great* things without it[5]. Stress comes from the Latin word *stringere*, which means to be drawn tight. Hans Selye (1907-1982), who was an Austrian-Canadian endocrinologist of Hungarian origin, was the first to conduct research on stress as it relates to humans. Selye believed that stress itself doesn't kill or destroy; our *reactions* to stress, instead, kill and destroy.

There are some wonderful definitions of stress both in the research community as well as in other literature; for our discussions, I define stress as *the subjective experience of psychological and physical effects when we feel we're inadequate to the task or demand*. Stress is the result of the *subjective perception* of being weighed, being measured, and being found wanting. Physiologically, our bodies *thrive* on balance; *anything* that disrupts this balance becomes a *stressor* and sets off our internal stress alarm system. Stress, then, lets us know that something is off, and we need to do something about it.

Stressors. A stressor is any person, place or thing that signals a threat and triggers a psychological, behavioral, or physical response. Think of a stressor as an *allergen*; my wife Tabitha is allergic to pecan shells and I'm allergic to beef. Each of these foods triggers a response in our bodies as a way for the body to protect itself.

Just like pecan shells aren't an allergen for me and beef isn't an allergen for Tabitha, stressors impact people differently. Even within the same allergen, for example, some people have an *intense* or life-threatening reaction, while others have a *mild* and non-life-threatening reaction. A bee sting would be annoying, at best, for me; for Tabitha, however, we'd need an Epipen® to ensure she could breathe. As you can see, what may be a stressor to you, may not be a stressor to your coworkers, classmates, neighbors, or family members. Based on this example, I'm sure you can see that stressors *can* significantly impair optimal functioning.

When I was growing up in Zambia, a company called Speciality Foods made Proton Biscuits (cookies, for my American audience). They were the thin, crispy kind of biscuits. My brothers used to call me proton biscuit because I was thin as a rail and my pectoral muscles were the size of proton biscuits...*allegedly*. While stressors can be seen as an allergen, we can also think of them as *resistance*. In order to develop pectoral muscles, or any other muscle, we need resistance. The moment we begin movements appropriate to developing a muscle, we're stressing that muscle — causing muscle tissue to tear and new muscle tissue to grow. That's how you go from having proton biscuits to having ciabatta rolls for pecs. For muscles to grow, they need stressors; to have stressors, we need stress. That's why a simplified and single vision of stress is dangerous...

Binary Stress. I was in undergraduate school at Sam Houston State when I first developed the ability to effectively and verbally distinguish between good and bad stress. I never liked the idea of stress constantly getting a bad rap, especially when I found myself *thriving* because of stress — or was it in spite of stress? Anyway, I was taking a *Psychology of Adjustment* course, and was able to finally put the argument to rest because stress branches off into the binary of *eustress* and *distress*.

Eustress is good or positive stress. This is the kind of stress that brings focus, facilitates the completion of important tasks, as well as activates and motivates us towards achievement[6]. Eustress results from the balance between *hyperstress* (which is over stress) and *hypostress* (which is under stress)[7]. Think of lifting weights in the gym: hyperstress would be attempting to lift 600 pounds when you're not able, and hypostress would be lifting 5 pounds when you're able to lift more. Neither scenario would bring desired outcomes; unless, of course, you planned on being injured or not growing your muscles. We need eustress to help us grow — our muscles as well as our minds, hearts, eyes, etc.

Distress, on the other hand, is bad and unproductive stress. It dampens spirits, thwarts accomplishment[8], and is the reason stress, as a whole, gets a bad rap. When most people think about stress, they often mean distress. Distress occurs the moment we step past the threshold of eustress; it's a deviation from the healthy confines of physiological, psychological, and behavioral functioning.

As I'm sure you see, I'm leading you towards a different perspective concerning stress. Stress may, indeed, be the big, bad wolf trying to blow your proverbial house down — that's one perspective; if we put on the right glasses, however, we may be able to see that stress also forces us to fortify our homes — the result being that we're stronger than ever and more capable after stress.

This perspective essentially sees our problem *not* with stress itself, but with how we *choose* to *adapt* to it. The reality is that the threat and risk of stress can never be *eliminated*; what we *can* do is *mitigate* the risks of stress with preparedness. In the same way we can't stop a hurricane, but can be prepared for it, we can *diminish* the effects of distress and *maximize* the effects of eustress with the kind of preparedness that resiliency affords.

3 Tools for Your Toolbox

1. Stress is necessary for a meaningful life.
2. My reaction to stress gives it direction.
3. Stress teaches me to be prepared.

3. Positive Psychology

A PESSIMIST SEES THE DIFFICULTY IN EVERY OPPORTUNITY;
AN OPTIMIST SEES THE OPPORTUNITY IN EVERY DIFFICULTY.
Winston Churchill

Galen, a Greek physician who practiced in Rome in the First Century, was called to attend to the wife of a Roman aristocrat. Her doctor had been treating her for an organic complaint, but she hadn't improved. Galen, while taking her pulse, mentioned the name of an actor with whom her name was linked in the gossip of the town. Her pulse immediately bounded. Then Galen leaned down and whispered something in her ear that made her laugh. That laugh began her cure and is one of the earliest instances of a psychiatric treatment for psychosomatic illness[1].

Before I became a practicing performance psychologist, my official title was *Behavioral Scientist*. Most people cringe when they hear the word psychologist. It happens to me all the time: I meet people and they ask what I do. I tell them I'm a performance psychologist and work in an idea studio that uses behavioral science to help people thrive. Their brains usually shut off after the word *psychologist*, as the rest of my words disappear into a fog. Some people manage to ask what a performance psychologist does, but usually people clamp up because they think I'll start analyzing them. Thing is, I've already analyzed them! So, when *you* think of psychology, what comes to mind? It is positive? Negative? Pretty much the same as when you hear the word stress?

Our view of stress has been largely influenced by our general view of psychology. The *deficit* model of psychology — the idea that we can learn about thriving by studying failure — has ruled much of our thinking about psychology. I hated the prospect of learning about dysfunction in my psychology classes in undergrad because the constant focus was on what was *broken*. I didn't understand how we were supposed to learn about success, thriving, and being whole from a focus on human pathology. I must have been onto something because as I was wondering this, so was Dr. Martin E.P. Seligman.

Positive psychology is a relatively new branch of psychology that began with Dr. Seligman using his 1998 address as then-President of the American Psychological Association to highlight the imbalance in psychology, with its focus on disorder and deficits. Seligman believed that it was important to go beyond studying weakness and damage by including the study of strength and virtue. His view of psychological treatment was going beyond fixing what is broken by nurturing what is best within us. Because of Seligman's research and address, Division 17 of the American Psychological Association was born; a division focused on positive psychology.

Seligman and his Harvard colleague Csikszentmihalyi argued, in their 2000 seminal paper on positive psychology, that since World War II, psychology had become a science driven by the disease model of repairing human damage, yet psychologists knew very little about how people flourish. Allow me to give you a short history lesson and I'll move on — I promise. Before World War II, psychology developed three missions: *curing mental illness*; *helping people have a more productive and satisfying life*; and, *identifying and nurturing individual talent*[2]. Unfortunately, two things happened to limit the last two parts of the mission: in 1946, the Veteran's Administration was created, with several psychologists focusing their efforts on the treatment of mental illness; then in 1947, the National Institutes of Mental Health was founded, making the study of pathology a key focus area[3]. Because of this, curing mental illness took priority – especially with many veterans returning from World War II hurting – while helping people thrive, identify and nurture their individual talents became a low priority.

Fortunately, Seligman, and many other researchers, including yours truly, have, for the past 20 years, been adding to the growing body of research focusing on what makes us thrive. Positive psychology has become one of the fastest growing branches of psychology. To be clear, positive psychology isn't a feel-good and rosy view on life. Positive psychology researchers and practitioners don't neglect the negative and accentuate only the positive; we try, instead, to bring balance by making sure that what makes us great is spoken for just as much as what ails and confounds us.

While there are several good definitions of positive psychology, I like the simplicity of the one proposed by the International Positive Psychology Association: *The scientific study of what enables individuals and communities to thrive.* This definition aligns with my personal and professional belief in the inherent goodness within us. As Reeve put it: Positive psychologists look at an individual and wonder "what could be" while realizing that people fall short of "what could be"[4].

Positive psychology is the lens through which I view stress; not only because there are no better alternatives, but also because the popular perspective is clearly not working. I have yet to meet a client that can *sustainably* use the deficit model and thrive long-term. Positive psychology is not blind to the realities of life and circumstances; the difference lies in what positive psychology *does* with the realities of life and circumstances.

As you'll learn in the chapters that follow, circumstances are *neutral*; they are neither positive nor negative. They become positive or negative based on the lens through which we view them. I've come to learn that circumstances and the realities of life often *conspire* to show us what we're made of. Like teabags, we haven't the faintest clue of the aroma and flavor of the tea until the teabags are dropped in hot water. The positive psychologist doesn't complain about being drowned in scalding water; instead, the positive psychologist says, "Finally, everyone will know just how *aromatic* and *flavorful* I am!"

3 Tools for Your Toolbox

1. I will nurture what's great within me.
2. I will develop a healthy disregard for the impossible.
3. Circumstances are neutral; I direct them.

4. Posttraumatic Growth

DIFFICULT ROADS OFTEN LEAD TO BEAUTIFUL DESTINATIONS.
Anonymous

A month and a day after my 16th birthday, the worst of mankind was unleashed as approximately 800,000 Tutsis, Twa, and moderate Hutus were murdered during the Rwandan genocide. Most of the images we got in Zambia weren't sanitized as would be done here in the States. To a young and impressionable mind, the images were nothing short of horrific and send a chill down my spine, even as I write this. Movies such as *Hotel Rwanda* and books such as Immaculée Ilibagiza's *Left to Tell* and Jeanne Celestine Lakin's *A Voice in the Darkness* tell the lived experience of surviving genocide against incredible odds.

I recently had the pleasure of sharing the stage with Jeanne Celestine Lakin at a conference. She is a beautiful soul, both inside and out, and her warmth touched me in ways that continue to ripple in my life even to this writing. I find myself deeply enriched by her and her experience. Enriched by her experience? Yes, enriched. Those words would seem odd, even hollow, if not for Jeanne's perspective that staying alive through this horrific experience allowed her to see the complete lesson that pain had to teach her. Coming from a person whose country, world, and family were decimated, you can see how Jeanne represents enrichment to me and to anyone else willing to listen. She's so positive!

Survivors of genocide, sexual assault, and other trauma experience *immense* and *intense* stress during and after trauma. Studies have shown that experiencing this level of stress can lead to negative outcomes. For Jeanne, though she had to do the work of healing, her experience of genocide led to positive outcomes. My shameless plug here is for you to pick up her book and learn how. Jeanne experienced a horrific and terrifying trauma that completely disrupted her life, but her focus turned out to be on learning what the pain of her experience was trying to teach her. Absolutely fascinating!

Now that we've discussed the binary of stress and the value of seeing stress through a positive psychology lens, we can discuss two *positive* outcomes of stress. To reiterate, stress *can* have deleterious effects on us physiologically, psychologically, and behaviorally. Many studies, as well as yours and my own personal experiences, have shown us that prolonged exposure to stress can lead to negative outcomes including illnesses such as heart disease and ulcers. Stress, as we can see from Jeanne's perspective, can also lead to positive outcomes; one of which is posttraumatic growth (PTG).

The experience of suffering is generally universal, and creates a paradox: on one hand, there are negative psychological, physiological, and behavioral effects; on the other, the experience can generate meaningful outcomes[1]. Some people emerge from trauma having experienced positive changes in spite of the distress caused by traumatic events. Researchers have found that adversity and suffering have the potential to facilitate growth and development across the lifespan, especially since they may facilitate stronger *meaning-making* and *maturity* in us[2].

Historically, the study of exposure to trauma has been filtered through the deficit model — researchers have focused on the negative outcomes of trauma, especially the ubiquitous posttraumatic stress disorder (PTSD). Let me be clear: the evidence pointing to the many negative physiological, psychological, and behavioral consequences produced by traumatic events is staggering. There is, however, another side to the coin; and significant research is giving credence to the positive aspects of the posttraumatic experience.

Around the time that Dr. Seligman was giving his field-changing address to the APA, and I was frustrated by the incessant focus on brokenness in psychology, Dr. Richard Tedeschi and Dr. Lawrence Calhoun were popularizing posttraumatic growth (a term they coined only a few years earlier). Posttraumatic growth refers to the positive change that occurs as a result of encountering significant adversity. Posttraumatic growth explains why some people's struggle with stressful and traumatic events can lead to positive outcomes such as positive changes in identity, priorities, and relationships[3].

According to Tedeschi and Calhoun, posttraumatic growth is both a *process* and an *outcome*; it develops from our engagement with complex emotional, social, and cognitive variables that can enrich our well-being and life satisfaction after trauma. Researchers have found that some of the benefits after trauma include greater self-efficacy (which is feelings of personal capability), changes in our general approach to life, a greater appreciation for life, and, my favorite, an increased awareness of new possibilities. Posttraumatic growth serves as an umbrella term for the *benefits*, *meaning-making*, and *growth* that can follow adversity[4].

The theme of suffering and adversity leading to growth is not new. Tedeschi and Calhoun admitted that the view that people can change, sometimes radically, by experiencing and enduring life's challenges or suffering is age-old. Examples pre-dating Tedeschi and Calhoun's work abound, including Friedrich Nietzsche's famous quote: "That which does not kill us makes us stronger." The Apostle Paul, as far back as 50AD, wrote in his letter to the Romans: We can rejoice, too, when we run into problems and trials, for we know that they help us develop endurance. And endurance develops strength of character, and character strengthens confident hope of salvation[5]. The hero-journey, where some quest begins with hardship and suffering but leads to victory and triumph, has been part of human art and literature for thousands of years[6]. *The Count of Monte Cristo* (circa 1844), my favorite Alexandre Dumas novel, is just one of many pieces of literature that exemplifies hardship leading to triumph.

Perhaps the most meaningful example of how trauma and suffering can trigger a process of positive transformation comes from the 1946 book, *Man's Search for Meaning*. In it, Dr. Viktor Frankl, neurologist and psychiatrist as well as Auschwitz survivor, described personal transformation similar to posttraumatic growth that is set in motion by unfair and unjust circumstances. Frankl showed us how an existential understanding of suffering can be a potent tool for not just coping with trauma but emerging from trauma stronger and more capable.

The key contributions Tedeschi and Calhoun made to our understanding of trauma and suffering are (a), the creation of a systematic process for studying growth after trauma; and, (b), narrative transformation as a result of trauma. Because of Tedeschi and Calhoun, we now have a burgeoning field of study that investigates the personal transformation that occurs in the aftermath of personal tragedy and trauma. Researchers have conducted studies across ages, cultures, genders, types of trauma, and much more; this has led to a deeper understanding of the net-positive effects of trauma.

The most significant contribution Tedeschi and Calhoun made to our understanding of trauma and suffering, in my very biased opinion, is the idea of *narrative transformation* as a result of trauma. My opinion is biased because (a), I'm a phenomenologist — I traffic in narrative and the lived experience of others; (b), I've been studying the power of story for a decade and a half; and (c), I've found that the words that do the most damage are often the ones we *don't* say, but ruminate on. I'm getting ahead of myself. Suffice it to say that trauma need not lead to posttraumatic stress disorder or posttraumatic stress syndrome. It *can* lead to posttraumatic growth and resiliency. I'd like to show you how…

3 Tools for Your Toolbox

1. Suffering can make me or break me; the choice is mine.
2. Adversity can positively change my story.
3. Challenges can be the turning point of my life.

5. Resiliency

GRACE UNDER PRESSURE IS RARELY INBORN OR GOD-GIVEN.
THE ONLY WAY TO MEET THE CHALLENGE OF OPTIMAL
PERFORMANCE IS TO TRAIN – MENTALLY, PHYSICALLY, AND
EMOTIONALLY – EVERY DAY OF YOUR LIFE.
Author Unknown

I attended two of Zambia's premier schools: Namununga from first to seventh grade, and Lake Road from eighth to twelfth grade. Small cohort sizes, no larger than 50, meant it took a lot to get into these schools and you had to bring it each term because private school wasn't cheap. I can't think of a time when academic achievement and competition was fiercer than those twelve years of school. Each term, we were ranked in not just our entire grade, but each class and in each subject.

I would score 99% in a subject and be ranked 9th in one subject or score 95% and be ranked 6th in another subject. From first to twelfth grade, I never ranked higher than 6th in the grade and 3rd in my class. There was pressure to perform at the highest levels because my parents were shelling out a small fortune for my private education and my teachers, who were among the best in the country, were pouring themselves into me so that I'd thrive one day.

I wish I could say that I was a bright student; I wasn't. School didn't come easy for me, but it didn't come hard for me either. Every academic achievement since first grade was hard-fought and hard-earned. I began first grade as a five-year-old battling with peers who were six and seven years old. My parents, and my teachers, never once cared; they expected results and demanded my utmost. And that's been my story since that January in 1984 when I began first grade at Namununga — I've had to muster the courage and extra effort to win.

My mother would rip pages out of my books, even though the work was completed correctly, because she didn't think my handwriting was clean or clear enough. She expected both the *delivery* and the *content* to be appropriate.

Traumatic at times, those experiences taught me to develop resiliency and find the reserve energy needed to accomplish whatever task or goal before me. Most of all, those early experiences taught me that resiliency is not a gift or an inheritance; it's something we *earn* after being battle-tested.

Posttraumatic growth is one *positive* path branching out from eustress; the other is resiliency. As mentioned earlier, we can't develop resiliency without stress or trauma; as a matter of fact, resiliency is the variable that can moderate the effects of stress[1]. In other words, resiliency is the *inoculation* we need against the negative effects of future stress! I'm obviously getting too excited and ahead of myself, so let's talk about what resiliency is…

Resiliency is our ability to meet stress and adversity head-on, and adapt[2]. Resiliency doesn't imply that we won't be tested; it does imply, however, that we have the mental, spiritual, and other fortitude to appropriately assess our circumstances, overcome them, and, at the very least, return to normalcy. Life can sometimes be a crucible; a place of severe testing where concentrated forces meet to effect change. Severe testing is an opportunity for feedback; it let's us know our mettle and generates a grade report of our capabilities. Such tests are vital to motivation as they provide the feedback we need to know if we're on the right track in terms of our readiness for challenges. Surprises are the new normal, and resiliency is the skill necessary for appropriately handling stress and surprises[3].

Before I share my definition of resiliency, I need to give you another brief history lesson. It'll be very brief, I promise. Resiliency research occurs in four waves. The first wave focuses on describing resilient qualities — what we, in the business, call *protective factors*. This wave of research leads to a list of protective factors that help us *grow* through adversity (not just "go" through it). The second wave of resiliency research focuses on understanding the *processes* that lead to resiliency. This wave brings us a description of the disruptive and reintegrative process of *acquiring* protective factors. The third wave combines what we learn from the first two waves and focuses on what *facilitates* resiliency; that is, the driving forces within us that lead us towards resiliency. The fourth wave of resiliency research integrates neuroscience, behavioral science, and the life sciences to gain a more holistic and multifaceted view of resiliency. In this wave, we gain a better understanding of how multiple systems interact to shape the development of resiliency.

If you're paying close attention to the tenses in the previous paragraph, you'll notice that I used present tense for each wave; that's because these waves are *concurrent* as researchers continue their work in each of the waves at the same time. In case you wanted to know, my focus area is the second wave — I want to know *how* we can acquire protective factors to inoculate us against the negative effects of stress.

Researchers have defined resiliency as robustness, the ability to cope with stress, adapting to stress, and more. Interestingly, most definitions of resiliency revolve around "bouncing back." It makes sense since, etymologically, resiliency finds its roots from the Latin verb *resilire*, which means to rebound or leap back. Resiliency draws its meaning even further from the Latin word *resiliens*, which means recovery and reorganizing.

One last distinction I'd like to make before I share my definition of resiliency is in the use of the word resiliency, rather than resilient or resilience. Instead of saying someone *is* resilient, I say they *have* resiliency; this is because, in my own research, and countless hours poring over others' research, I've found that we can *possess* and *nurture* amazing qualities such as resiliency. My focus is on *possession* and *nurturing*; in other words, I'd like to *have* and *develop* resiliency rather than *be* resilient. Taking *ownership* of and *developing* resiliency is open to all; it's not a special gift based on genetics or other endowments.

While research has shown that some personality types are more predisposed to resiliency, resiliency is not only a function of genetics; resiliency *can* be learned and taught! Coming from the Second Wave of Resiliency Research perspective, I want to help you and others acquire protective factors that will help you constantly develop and nurture resiliency.

My definition of resiliency is greatly influenced by something that happened during the early days of resiliency research in the 1970s. Norman Garmenzy is considered by most to be the pioneer of resiliency research. In his groundbreaking work with schizophrenics, he found that, though faced with difficult circumstances, some of the adult schizophrenics he worked with functioned well — holding down jobs, maintaining romantic relationships, and keeping their activities in good order. Unfortunately, because the focus was on the strength and fortitude of his research subjects, the media began to call these subjects "super kids" and "vulnerable but invincible"[4].

Ann Masten, Garmenzy's protégé, would have none of this "extraordinary" nonsense. Masten believed that resiliency is a common phenomenon that occurs when basic human adaptational systems are in optimal operation[5]. Masten's research found that resiliency is not the domain of extraordinary people, but quite commonplace. The title of her seminal paper, *Ordinary Magic*, illustrates not only her conviction but the commonality of resiliency. This historical background greatly informs and influences my definition of resiliency because resiliency is open to all who are willing to do the psychological and behavioral work to *acquire* it. Resiliency isn't something you *have*; it's something you *tap into*.

That said, here's my long-awaited definition of resiliency: *the ability to experience disruption and return from it armed with additional protective factors and higher levels of functioning.* To put this definition into context, how would you react to a cancer diagnosis? To the loss of a very close loved one? To failing a class, just short of graduation? To breaking up with someone you were sure was your mate for life? Most definitions of resiliency say you'd do well to simply return to normalcy — to where you were before the disruption. I'm not sure about you, but I have no interest in going ten rounds with cancer only to come to the other side the same as I was when I entered the ring! I want to not only kick cancer in the teeth, but also takes its sandwich *and* the bag of Cheetos®! I want to emerge from the experience wiser, kinder, stronger, more focused, more compassionate, and so on. Returning to baseline is overrated! I want to *raise* the baseline! As Flach put it, we should emerge better put together and more qualified to deal with life's challenges *because* of our experience[6].

As you'll learn in the next chapter, we have *choices* when we encounter disruption; we have distinct paths we can take during and after disruption. The path we take will ultimately determine whether we collect protective factors along the way that'll become armor against *future* disruption. If stress is the payment we must all make to live on earth, I plan on meeting it armed with every tool I need to reduce its negative effects.

This brings up an important and crucial pillar of resiliency: *self-efficacy*. Self-efficacy is the belief that individual action can influence circumstances[7]. Self-efficacy is a cognitive theory developed by Albert Bandura in 1977; the theory asserts that we can make behavioral changes if we believe that we either have the abilities to perform a task or the capacity to learn behaviors that are essential to reaching our goals. With self-efficacy, we not only *recognize* that we have a choice when disruption visits us but can also call upon specific skills and tools to meet the disruption with confidence.

3 Tools for Your Toolbox

1. Resiliency is the antidote to stress.
2. Resiliency is something I can and must learn.
3. Resiliency is work with immeasurable rewards.

6. Disruption & Reintegration

EVERYONE HAS A PLAN
UNTIL THEY GET PUNCHED IN THE MOUTH.
Mike Tyson

When I was a child growing up in Zambia, I thought it odd that my parents focused a great deal on preparing me and my eight siblings for the future. My mother would say, "*When* you face this challenge, respond this way." My father would say, "You'll understand *when* you're a dad." I don't remember either of them using the word "if" in these types of teaching moments. In my little mind, it was a foregone conclusion that what they said was sure to happen, so I needed to be ready for it.

Just as my parents prepared me to face the world without them close to guide me, I'd like to prepare you by sharing an important reality: it's not a matter of *if* the storm will come in your life, it's a matter of *when*. Besides never getting out of life alive — come on, that's just funny, and you need to lighten up! — we *never* get through life without experiencing storms. Part of my work as a performance psychologist is to prepare my clients for the inevitable. When we know that something is inevitable, we can muster the physiological, psychological, and behavioral resources to meet the eventuality with courage, focus, dignity, grace, self-compassion, and strength.

To effectively and constantly find the courage and strength to meet life's storms, we need a model that can help us cognitively *illustrate* and *evaluate* our circumstances. The best model I've found comes to us courtesy of the late psychiatrist, Dr. Frederic Flach, who detailed his findings on resiliency in his 1988 book, *Resilience: Discovering a New Strength at Times of Stress*. In this classic, he describes *The Law of Disruption and Reintegration*, which we'll add to our toolbox for developing and nurturing resiliency.

Our Comfort Zone. Flach believed that all living structures have an inherent power and need to preserve states of relative coherence. Homeostasis, if you remember from your biology class, is a biological *imperative* to maintain the status quo, or to regain it when it's been lost[1]. Many life events are stressors that often blindside us or force us out of our comfort zone. This comfort zone is something Flach called our *biopsychospiritual homeostasis*. Our biopsychospiritual homeostasis is the main target of all stressors. Just like the thief comes only to steal, kill, and destroy[2], stressors are on a search-and-destroy mission to disrupt, damage, or destroy our biopsychospiritual homeostasis.

Our biopsychospiritual homeostasis is very important because our human nature dictates that we are constantly adapted spiritually, mentally, and physically to the good or bad circumstances in our lives. Recent research has renamed this state of equilibrium *ecobiopsychospiritual* homeostasis to include ecological homeostasis, which is adapting to where and how we live, work, and play. Put together, our ecobiopsychospiritual homeostasis allows us to function with a relative sense of *predictability*.

While many of us think we don't follow a routine, our lives are built *on* and *by* routine. We tend to chew the same way, walk the same way, wake up the same way, sleep the same way, and so much more. How do we know when something's off? When we're chewing differently after dental work, walking differently after an injury, or wake up in a fright after a nightmare. I could go into the neuroscience of why this is, but I promised not to get too technical, so I'll keep my word. Just know that routine isn't necessarily a bad thing; it's a biological *need*.

Breaking the Comfort Zone Barrier. While serving a legitimate ecobiopsychospiritual need, *comfort zones don't make for the best places for growth*. Each time we need to learn something new, meet someone new, or go somewhere new, we have to break the barrier of our comfort zone. For many of us, this can be *daunting*, to put it mildly. In order for us to acquire and refine protective factors, we have to experience disruption.

In order to destabilize ecobiopsychospiritual homeostasis, bifurcation points are necessary[3]. Bifurcation points are moments in life when major shifts occur, and is a

43

term derived from the language of contemporary physics to represent times of extreme change. Bifurcation points are like crucibles, which I mentioned earlier; crucibles are places where concentrated forces meet to create change. During bifurcation, destabilization may lead our internal and external structure into chaos, with the outcomes being rather unpredictable[4]. We may remain forever destabilized, form new homeostasis around poor coping behavior, or, under the best circumstances, the stage may be set for us reintegrate into more effective levels of personal coherence[5].

Flach described *disruption* as the result of life events which throw us out of ecobiopsychospiritual homeostasis. Bifurcation points lead to disruption, which is the outcome of being blindsided by life events or stepping out of our comfort zone. Remember: *every time something important must be learned, especially if it goes against one or more of our presumptions, disruption must occur*[6].

Think of disruption as the *key* that unlocks innate resiliency because, by nature, *there's no demand for improvement and growth while we're in ecobiopsychospiritual homeostasis.* Opportunities abound just outside our comfort zone; but only if we escape its prison. Sadly, staying imprisoned by comfort is a safer bet than enduring the unpredictability of stepping out of our ecobiopsychospiritual homeostasis.

Initially, Flach viewed disruption as being confined to major bifurcation points in life. In my research, I found that some researchers narrowly defined resiliency as a result of "extreme" stress or disruption. Fortunately, after further examination, Flach discovered that bifurcation points occur regularly throughout our lifecycle as we pass from one phase of life to another[7]. He found that disruption is a *repetitive* cycle that presents in both significant and mundane aspects of our daily life. As you'll learn in Part II, *waiting to develop or nurture resiliency when a major life event occurs is too late. To be ready for the major, we have to allow the minor to prepare us.*

The Arthey Story

Chris and Denise were British expatriates working for an oil and gas company in Houston, Texas. Over time, their English charm and deep spirituality won me over, and we became close. I had them over for dinner one evening, and two days later they were involved in a near-fatal accident that left them maimed. A drunk driver swerved into their lane, hit multiple vehicles head-on, including Chris and Denise while they were riding a motorcycle. Were it not for Chris's riding skills, I'd be writing about their passing.

Chris and Denise had their left legs amputated from the knee down. Chris cycled and ran long-distance before the accident. In his 50s at the time, he'd been running marathons and other races all over the world for years. For most people, this blow would've crushed them. I was there during their rehab and I've never seen a more positive and deeply circumspect example of experiencing disruption. With each visit, Chris and Denise gained not only physical strength, but deeper spiritual focus; their infectious grace, astounding before the accident, became, well, pandemic!

There's so much more to their story but, get this: They *forgave* the driver! Chris still cycles and runs long-distance. He's dubbed himself "the one-legged wonder," retired, went back to college, speaks to companies about safety, and is a tester for a major prosthetic company in England.

Do you think their resiliency was a *result* of the accident, or was it being developed prior? As you rightly guessed, they were allowing the minor to prepare them long before the accident. With each frustration, they built their defense system. With each challenge, they fortified their proverbial city. With each obstacle, they deepened their resolve.

Life After Disruption. Flach viewed disruption as an opportunity to discover new coping mechanisms, to reform our view of the world and ourselves — a process he called *reintegration*. Reintegration is the process of putting the pieces of ourselves and our worlds back together after disruption. Reintegration is the ability to *reconfigure* ourselves after bifurcation so as to achieve *perspective*; leading to new and more meaningful levels of structure and understanding[8]. Once disruption occurs, reintegration — that is, reestablishing homeostasis — becomes a biological imperative. Flach's model is a tool we can use to adapt to disruptions and choose the *outcomes* of these disruptions.

I love options. Most of us complain about too many options and don't appreciate them until we don't have them. Because of my bent towards self-efficacy, I appreciate it when I can psychologically, physiologically, and behaviorally impact my circumstances (or the experience of them). Reintegration comes with options. Understanding the disruptive and reintegrative process that follows every adversity or new life experience gives us the opportunity to map our life experiences with resiliency[9]. According to Flach's model, when faced with disruption, we reintegrate from bifurcation in one of four ways: *dysfunctionally, with loss, homeostatically,* or *resiliently.*

Dysfunctional reintegration, as the name suggests, is marked by destructive behavioral patterns. This type of reintegration occurs when we envision possible identities that could help us reintegrate resiliently, but we resort to tools that are not progressive[10]. When we reintegrate dysfunctionally, we may resort to disruptive behaviors such as violence or substance abuse to deal with adversity[11]. Excessive drinking after a breakup or job loss and isolation or checking-out after the loss of a loved one are two examples of dysfunctional reintegration.

Reintegration with loss happens when we lose critical protective factors and emerge from disruption with lowered homeostasis. This path of reintegration has us faring lower than we were prior to the disruption. Often, when we reintegrate with loss, we experience life events with no openness to the insights such events bring[12]. So, what do we do? We give up hope, drive, and motivation because the demands of the disruption are too high.

Homeostatic reintegration is essentially zero-sum. We neither lose nor gain protective factors as we deal with disruption[13]. This version of reintegration has us ignoring the insights and directions received as we process disruption. When this path is chosen, we give up and go back to what we know, even if it may be undesirable[14]. Reintegrating homeostatically maintains the previous comfort level[15] and is often simply about healing and getting over a disruption[16] rather than attempting to grow from it[17].

Resilient reintegration is the ideal form of reintegration. When we resiliently reintegrate, we gain additional protective factors as we deal with disruption. Resilient reintegration leads to higher levels of homeostasis[18]. Resilient reintegration is *additive*, and results in personal growth, increased knowledge and self-understanding, and the acquisition of additional protective factors[19]. Without resilient reintegration, the same disruptions keep coming because we've not acquired the protective factors necessary to handle the disruption. Resilient reintegration gives us the opportunity for growth, development, and skill-building[20].

Disruption is *inevitable*; we do, however, have a choice as to which levels of coherence we'll be when we reintegrate. Flach's *Law of Disruption and Reintegration* is important to all our lives. According to Flach:

o   In order to learn and to experience meaningful change, we must fall apart.

o   During periods of chaos, we're at varying degrees of risk, as we can't determine in advance what direction our future will take.

o   By making us more knowledgeable and adaptive, each period of disruption and reintegration is necessary to prepare us to meet the stresses that lie ahead.

o   Failure to pass successfully through any stress cycle can leave us crippled, without the strengths we'll need when other bifurcation points appear.

Resiliently reintegrating allows us to build *capacity* by gaining more tools to face future disruption. While the realities dictate that we may not follow this path every time, it should be the path we strive for with each passing disruption. Let me be clear: unless we learn how to handle minor disruptions like being cut off in traffic, for example, we haven't a hope of resiliently reintegrating when major storms come.

3 Tools for Your Toolbox

1.   I have what it takes to meet the inevitable.
2.   Only outside my comfort zone can I grow.
3.   If I master the small challenges, big ones won't crush me.

PART II

As a phenomenologist, I interview people to learn about their *lived* experiences. Rather than using a survey with predetermined responses, I dig deep into the stories of those I'm fortunate to interview. From these stories, *themes* emerge; it's these themes that inform my understanding of the concept under study.

In this part of the book, I'll share some of the themes that emerged from my most recent study on resiliency with organizational leaders. Please note that just because my research volunteers were organizational leaders doesn't mean this research has no value for someone who isn't an organizational leader. These leaders were mums and dads, neighbors and friends…just like you. All we did was limit their stressor to a recent one in the workplace.

For this study, I was interested in learning more about the types of narratives they (a) told *themselves*, (b) told *others*, and (c) told *about their circumstances*, as they experienced disruption and resiliently reintegrated. From this study, and many others in the field, it's very clear that narrative plays a very crucial role in the development of resiliency and the experience of posttraumatic growth.

If you remember, posttraumatic growth is essentially a *narrative transformation*. Hildon and his research team found that resiliency is impacted by the *types* of narratives people tell themselves and others in the face of adversity. This section of the book focuses on our storytelling. For better or worse, words — spoken and unspoken — are extremely powerful, especially in light of *developing* and *nurturing* resiliency.

7. The Power of Narrative

AN AUTHENTIC AND HONEST BRAND NARRATIVE IS FUNDAMENTAL TODAY; OTHERWISE, YOU WILL SIMPLY BE EDITED OUT.
Marco Bizzarri

There's a Persian story of a king who found out that his first wife was unfaithful to him. After this experience, he decided to marry a new wife each day and behead her the next day — thus ensuring she had no opportunity to be unfaithful to him. Against her father's wishes, Scheherazade became wife number 1,002, as the king had killed 1,001 wives by the time he married Scheherazade. That night, she asked the king if she might say goodbye to her sister who'd been conscripted to ask Scheherazade to tell her a story.

Scheherazade was a keen and shrewd storyteller! The king lay awake all night listening in amazement to Scheherazade's tale until she stopped midway through the story. When he asked her to finish the story, she told him it was late; he spared her life so she could finish the story the next evening. The next day, she finished the story and began another one; this one even more riveting than the first. As happened the night before, she stopped in the middle and the king spared her life to finish the story the next day. As the story goes, the king spared Scheherazade day after day as he eagerly awaited the completion of the previous night's story. At the end of 1,001 nights and 1,000 stories, Scheherazade told all the stories she had; during that time, the king had fallen deeply in love with Scheherazade — he spared her life and made her his queen.

Coming from a culture that holds history in the palm of its stories, I can relate to the pull of great storytelling. Whether or not you come from a culture of storytelling, your brain is made for story — it's simply the best way for the brain to impose structure and logic to the seemingly random nature of human experience. Untold and unfinished stories are the ultimate brain-freeze; we know that something is missing and have to remedy it.

What kind of storyteller are *you*? Can you hold *yourself* down with a *riveting* tale in the same way Scheherazade did? Will you take an honest inventory of your life and assign appropriate meaning to your contextual experiences? These are important questions because they bear on whether or not resiliency is a skill you'll develop. To become a good storyteller, you have to understand that:

> Story is everywhere. Your body tells a story. The smile or frown on your face, your shoulders thrust back in confidence or slumped roundly in despair, the liveliness or fatigue in your gait, the sparkle of hope and joy in your eyes or the blank stare, your fitness, the size of your gut, the tone and strength of your physical being, your overall presentation — those are all part of your story, one that's especially apparent to everyone else.
>
> Your life is the most important story you will ever tell, and you're telling it right now, whether you know it or not. From very early on you're spinning and telling multiple stories about your life, publicly and privately, stories that have a theme, a tone, a premise — *whether you know it or not*. Some are for better, some for worse. No one lacks material. Everyone's got a story[1].

The most important thing about story is this: there's *no one* more qualified than *you* to tell it! As a performance psychologist, I can't tell my client's story better than they can. My job is to empower them and remind them that they can have a compelling and page-turning story. To do so, they must first have the *courage* to *tell* their story and, second, they must have the *boldness* to rewrite their story until it accurately reflects who they really are. As the *Spirit of the West* put it in the movie *Rango*: "No man can walk out of his own story."

Human beings are storytellers. We love a good narrative, especially one with multiple twists, plots, and subplots that keep us guessing. We use narrative to process our daily experiences. *Narratives are the running tales we use to experience, explore, and process our worldview*[2]. Narratives help us navigate our way through life by providing structure and direction, imposing meaning to the chaos, and giving context to our sensory experiences[3]. We were *made* for narrative! When adversity hits, however, the *direction* of our narratives is disrupted and how we respond to this disruption does a great deal to either fortify our resiliency or reveal the lack thereof[4]. As you'll probably tire of hearing me say, *storms come to reveal or increase our resiliency, or expose our lack of resiliency.*

For the past 16 years, I've been passionate about my story, others' story, and, most importantly, *how* we *tell* that story. Perhaps that's why I generally default to phenomenology as a research tool. Phenomenology is the study of the lived experiences of research participants. Participants tell their story, in their own words, and I get to go on the journey with them as they describe past experiences and how they felt, smelled, tasted, sounded, and so on. This would be creepy, if it weren't all done in the name of research...

A key part of our understanding and development of resiliency requires us to have an appreciation for the narrative we tell — to ourselves *and* to others. If you remember the chapter on Posttraumatic Growth, I mentioned that posttraumatic growth involves the powerful experience of *narrative transformation*. As humans, we assign *meaning* to adverse life events[5]. During bifurcation, people who resiliently reintegrate often construct narratives that *reinterpret* adversity[6]. This means that they look at their circumstances and draw *value* out of them, rather than blame their circumstances or see them as an impediment.

Cognitive Behavioral Therapy (CBT), my preferred therapeutic approach, helps clients understand how their thoughts and feelings influence their behavior. CBT challenges our assumptions and helps us expose the common cognitive and emotional *distortions* we make when under pressure. When viewed through CBT, we can see how thinking greatly influences feelings and actions, so that meaning is not static but can change based on how we assess and interpret unfolding events[7]. *The secret to achieving narrative transformation, and ultimately posttraumatic growth and resiliency, is learning how to assign appropriate meaning to life's events.*

Our behavior is greatly influenced by the scripts and narratives we tell, many of them having been chosen early in life and completely out of our conscious awareness[8]. The reality is that, when these scripts and narratives don't lead to desired outcomes, stress occurs; how we *reshape* our narratives is the difference between *surviving* and *thriving*[9]. As my definition of resiliency pointed out, it's not enough for us to merely survive the storm — though rebuild we must — we should emerge from the storm with additional protective factors and move to higher levels of functioning. Resiliency influences our appraisal of an event, which is often filtered by narratives and scripts[10]. In other words, we need resiliency to develop the ability to redirect our narrative; at the same time, we need to redirect our narrative in order for us to develop resiliency...

Do you see that the stories we tell ourselves greatly influence the mindset we have towards disruption? If our narrative is negative, defeatist, and victim-oriented, we'll see disruption as just another clear indication that we can never catch a break. If, on the other hand, our narrative is positive and focused on the growth opportunity, we'll see disruption as an opportunity to get tested on the material life has conspired to teach us since our last disruption. In the process, we're becoming more positive, collecting protective factors like Mario collects mushrooms, and arming ourselves for the next disruption. Put together, we emerge from disruption having resiliently reintegrated and refused to make waste of the opportunity that the disruption brought...

3 Tools for Your Toolbox

1. My story matters more than I often realize.
2. Resiliency is dependent on how I tell my story.
3. Narrative transformation makes adversity worth it.

8. The Narrative We Tell Ourselves

THE LANGUAGE USED IN TELLING OUR PERSONAL STORY AFFECTS US. WE REFLECT OUR MIND CHATTER.
Kilroy J. Oldster

Beethoven, the venerable composer, fired his housekeeper who'd taken excellent care of him because she once shielded him from an unpleasantness by fibbing about it. "Anyone who tells a lie hasn't a pure heart," he said, "and cannot make pure soup[1]." I've always said that I don't need protection from the world or from others; what I need protection from is myself! In my role as performance coach, I spend most of my time protecting my clients from themselves. Much of the pain we experience is a result of the battle we wage within. Think about it: we're our worst critics, we love to host pity parties, and we're adept at telling ourselves intricately-woven lies.

It's very hard to develop resiliency when the narrative I'm telling myself is distorted by lies or a victim-perspective. In order to effectively develop resiliency, I need to learn how to protect myself from *me*. First step? Acknowledge that I can be my own worst enemy, so I need to harness the greatness inside me and constantly expose the foolishness that makes me think it's okay to be a victim or lie to myself. Next, I need to learn how to use narrative appropriately. Narrative is an essential tool for meaning-making as we face disruption[2]. If we learn how to *tweak* the narrative, we can not only develop resiliency, we can also master our circumstances.

When I asked my research volunteers what types of narratives they told themselves as they faced stress and disruption, two themes emerged: first, they told themselves a *positive* narrative of the *future* and, second, they told themselves a *self-reflective* narrative of the *present*.

A Positively-Biased Narrative of the Future. As you may have guessed, I'm one of those annoyingly positive people.

53

When things go wrong, I tend to focus on *next* steps and how this setback has a hidden message that I need to discover. I'm enthusiastically optimistic and choose to see opportunity in all things. I don't thank God *for* everything, I thank God *in* everything. My personal brand of gratitude doesn't consider circumstances; whether or not things go my way, I'm grateful *in* everything. This is a deliberate *choice* I make, whatever my circumstances might be. I've chosen to take full ownership of my life; I have no control over *what* happens to me, but I have full control over *how* I respond. That attitude and mindset must be developed and nurtured before we experience disruption. Believing that we'll somehow draw out of a well with no resources when the disruption occurs is foolhardy. This is one of those lies I mentioned earlier; it's one of those lies that needs to be exposed daily. How? By calling it out and then choosing the direction of ownership concerning our reactions and responses to life's circumstances.

My research volunteers shared some heartfelt and difficult stresses and disruptions. To give you context, both male and female participants shed tears just thinking about what they went through. As expected, they experienced anger, hurt, insecurity, frustration, anxiety, and fear; what was inspiring about each of them is that they collectively focused on the positive outcomes *hidden* in their adversity. One participant fought the loss of identity by reminding herself that her worth as a woman and as a professional were not attached to the disruption she was experiencing. She reminded herself that she knew who she was and what she believed. Another participant told herself that she was the right person for the job, she was chosen for the job, she would successfully overcome the disruption, and ultimately do a great job. Another participant said, "I continued to tell myself that I could face whatever challenges were in front of me. The challenges would pass, and I would learn from them and be a better professional because of the experiences."

Would you echo their sentiments? Would you see what you're going through as an opportunity to emerge a better leader, spouse, friend, parent, neighbor, or human being? What kind of self-talk would you adopt? Would it be based on positivity and an encouraging, can-do attitude? Or would you invite yourself to another pity party?

Some of my research participants were flat-out done wrong! They had every right to put on the cloak of victimhood. Rather than stumble on the rock of offense, they lifted that rock, did some reps, and developed strength. What do *you* do with your rocks of offense? Do they become stumbling blocks or the weight you need for some deadlifts, arm curls, squats, and lunges?

I've known Dean and Luanne Johnson for almost 16 years. Among many other things in our time together, I've been blessed to watch their two children grow into funny, fun, and bright young people. My favorite childhood story of Perry goes like this: Luanne folded Perry's napkin during a meal differently than normal; she learned very quickly that this disruption was a bad idea. Perry threw a fit and commented: "I wish lightsabers were real!" This little guy was willing to go to insane lengths because his routine and expectation wasn't met! We're never going to let him live that one down!

Before you judge Perry, who's now a 20-year-old young man, just remember that, as adults, we're not much different than young Perry. When we're going through disruption, we often lose sight of reality. Perry was willing to use a lightsaber to get his mum to comply with folding his napkin the same way she always had. You and I are willing to use manipulation, anger, immaturity, and a host of other tools to bring back what we know rather than dance to the music of change.

As we go through disruption, we struggle with seeing the future clearly. We focus on all the permutations of things going wrong, when we should be enthusiastically overjoyed with where life might be taking us. I understand that such an attitude is learned; so, this is your opportunity to work on learning how to sometimes take the road in front of you with hope, a sense of humor, and positivity. Having a positive bias towards the future allows us to gain perspective and open ourselves up to possibility.

A Self-Reflective Narrative of the Present. I've been asked by audiences worldwide what one quality characterizes the most effective leader. Of course, that's not an easy question to answer since many leadership traits complement one another. After working with leaders of varying experience, across industries, and size of organization, I've found that the quality that exemplifies the most effective leader is a combination of self-awareness and self-reflection.

The New Oxford American Dictionary defines self-awareness as "conscious knowledge of one's own character, feelings, motives, and desires." Dictionary.com defines self-reflection as "the act of reflecting, as in casting back a light," "a fixing of the thoughts on something," and "careful consideration." To gain conscious knowledge of themselves, effective leaders shine a bright light on themselves, their thoughts, and their actions. They do this not so that everyone can see how great they are, but so that the darkness can be exposed. This quality enables leaders to be effective because it ensures that leaders are circumspect in what they do and who they are.

Self-reflection is a quality that ought to be adopted by all of us as it's central to worthy human experience. The Mishlei of Jewish Wisdom literature appropriately warns us: "Above everything else, guard your heart; for it is the source of life's consequences.[3]" The Contemporary English Version translates the warning as: "Carefully guard your thoughts because they are the source of true life.[4]" In ancient Jewish tradition, the heart was seen as the center of all thought and action.

Self-reflection is about ensuring that our thoughts, and subsequent actions, are aligned with our truest convictions. Effective leaders and effective human beings guard the sanctity of who they truly are by being self-reflective. They constantly shine a bright light on themselves, their thoughts, and their actions to make sure they align with who it is they are and want to be. As you might imagine, it was a thrill to see this theme emerge for my research participants...

Complementary to theme one, a positively-biased narrative of the future, theme two was a self-reflective narrative of the present. Participants took a *thoughtful* approach to what they were experiencing in the middle of their disruption, and what needed to be done to regain their balance. Participants looked inward for the resources they needed to appropriately process the disruption and resiliently reintegrate. Participants chose to shine a very bright light on themselves to expose hubris because, as one person put it, it wasn't about her but about her stakeholders.

Participants asked themselves hard and tough questions to make sure that each choice and decision made after the disruption was indicative of thoughtful consideration and devoid of knee-jerk emotional reactions. While they felt each emotion appropriately, they didn't allow emotions to cloud their judgment about who they were, what was really going on, and what needed to be done next.

What kind of narrative do *you* tell when hit by disruption? Do you dive headfirst into the deep end of emotions? Do you allow emotions to rule your decisions, or do you take a calm, collected, and reflective stance before making any decisions? Rather than focusing on what their disruption might have implied about them and their abilities, participants focused on the resources they had and who they were as individuals and as professionals. That kind of focus requires cognitive resources; the kind of resources that are often far from reach when we entertain emotions for too long.

I long each day to tell my story with authenticity. Anyone that's close to me knows that I feel very deeply and would be classified as an "emotional" person. My wife and loved ones get hugs and kisses from me constantly, I remind them how much I love them, and I'm always open to a heart-to-heart. Being self-reflective doesn't mean we have no emotions; that's virtually impossible, unless there's damage to the emotional center of the brain. There is, however, a place for emotions; resiliency is developed by understanding *how* and *when* to use emotions so that they become an asset instead of a liability. Being self-reflective includes knowing the power of emotions to help me make great decisions or to drag me into an abyss that yields very poor decisions.

We need to remember that the narrative we tell ourselves will impact the narrative we tell others. When we become adept at telling ourselves lies, it's easier for us to tell others lies. We lose authenticity when we constantly tell lies — no matter how small we think those distortions are. It's impossible to live a great life without authenticity. So, when we're telling ourselves a narrative that lacks appropriate positivity and self-reflection, we're forfeiting our best life because we're tarnishing ourselves with lie after lie.

3 Tools for Your Toolbox

1. A life well-lived requires authenticity.
2. Authenticity requires unvarnished truth.
3. Truth only exists when darkness is exposed.

9. The Narrative We Tell Others

THE MOST POWERFUL WORDS IN ENGLISH ARE,
"TELL ME A STORY."
Pat Conroy

While on vacation in Dublin, Ireland, Henry Ford was asked if he would contribute to a collection for a new orphanage. Judging the cause worthy, Ford promptly wrote out a check for £2,000. His generosity made headline news in the local paper the following day. The amount of the check, however, was wrongly quoted as £20,000. The director of the orphanage called on Ford at his hotel to apologize. "I'll phone the editor straight away and tell him to correct the mistake," he said. "There's no need for that," replied Ford, taking out his checkbook and pen. "I'll give you a check for the remaining eighteen thousand pounds, but only on one condition. When the new building opens, I want this inscription on it: I WAS A STRANGER, AND YOU TOOK ME IN[1]."

There's a glorious richness to our lives when we're other-oriented. Other-orientation is considering the thoughts, needs, motives, and desires of others before our own[2]. Other-orientation doesn't imply that we're weak and allow others to step all over us. Other-orientation is about the *direction* of our focus — *less* on the self, and *more* on others. It's a *perspective* that generates effective people and leaders because the person is driven by what's best for the team and others. It's a *mindset* that builds lifelong relationships with clients because the organization is, first and foremost, motivated by meeting clients' needs. And it's a *stance* that nurtures fruitful relationships and community because we find ways to meaningfully impact our children, friends, spouses, neighbors, and strangers.

As we experience disruption, we tell a clear and distinct narrative — verbally and non-verbally. How we carry ourselves as we experience disruption is a very loud nonverbal message to others. Whether we like it or not, people are always watching; how we carry ourselves becomes one of the most powerful messages we can send concerning our resiliency. The second-most powerful messages we send during disruption are verbal. While verbal messages are second-most powerful in terms of messages to others, they are just as damaging to us as a slouched demeanor. When adversity hits, and we're in the middle of challenging disruption, our body language can either augment our resiliency or show just how little we have.

When I asked my research participants what kind of narrative they told others as they went through disruption, they essentially said it was other-oriented. Participants' narrative gravitated towards others in their processing of their disruption. They focused on what others needed most, instead of what they were going through. Rather than drawing attention to the challenge and discomfort of their disruption, participants seemed to train their interpersonal processing of their disruption on how it affected others.

Let's pause for a brief moment and have an honest moment: Do you milk your disruptions for pity? Do you become self-focused when you're going through disruption? Do you draw attention to yourself and your circumstances every opportunity you get? Or, do you reframe your circumstances and do your best to stand tall?

There's no denying it: disruptions *suck*! They suck the air out of our lungs; and they suck the confidence right out of us. Fortunately, we're not without a remedy: we need to be bold in those moments and think about how our handling of the disruption affects others — especially those closest to us. There's no better example of resiliency than watching someone hold it together; not because they're being tough, but because they know that part of their growth is tied to their reactions. Responding poorly to disruption by whining, complaining, and making it about you doesn't create an atmosphere for growth; all it does is prolong the disruption because you've refused to grow. If, on the other hand, you experience disruption and make the choice to process the experience by reminding yourself and others that storms don't last, you gain perspective and have the bonus benefit of encouraging someone else. Instead of complaining, you could express how the pain is real, the discomfort is challenging, but you're focusing on the rewards of enduring. What would that do for your team, your family, and your community? Don't you think they'd be encouraged and emboldened to face change and uncertainty with courage?

My friend, it takes courage to live your best life. We step into the unknown every day. Our journey is filled with land mines. When one goes off, it's important to get some perspective and think about the impact your words, thoughts, and actions will have. Yes, a land mine just blew a big hole in your plans or life; that's your current reality, and something you now can't do anything about. What you *can* do is think about how that land mine can become an opportunity for you to grow and how your narrative of the experience can make a lasting impression on others.

My wife says I'm calm, even when land mines are going off all around me. I'm more like a duck; I may appear calm on the surface, but I'm paddling hard under the surface. In my case, however, I'm too lazy to exert myself when it doesn't add value; rather than try to be a tough guy, or pretend to play it cool, I'm paddling internally to make sure my emotions don't sabotage me. I'm doing my best to think long and hard about my next move. And I'm thinking about how my reaction *will* have an impact on my team, my family, and my community — I'm doing the work to make sure that the impact will be positive.

I'd like to give you some advice: when you're going through disruption, let your words be few. Nothing gets us into deeper trouble than a multitude of words when the rug has been pulled from under us. This is not the time for more words; this is the time to be measured. This is the time to ask ourselves hard questions, and to hold ourselves accountable for every last word. When we do, we begin to get centered and see things as they really are not as we fear them to be. We begin to maturely experience disruption and process it in a way that brings value to us and all who have the pleasure of living life with us. That, my friend, is how you develop resiliency: by doing the hard work that most people are simply unwilling to do.

1. During disruption, let your words be few.
2. It's not only about *you* during disruption; be other-oriented.
3. Resiliency takes a great deal of courage.

10. The Narrative We tell About Our Circumstances

CIRCUMSTANCES ARE BEYOND HUMAN CONTROL,
BUT OUR CONDUCT IS WITHIN OUR POWER.
Benjamin Disraeli

Nineteenth Century novelist and author of *Moby-Dick*, Herman Melville, was quite the storyteller. On a visit one evening to Nathaniel Hawthorne and his wife, Melville told them a story of a fight he'd witnessed on an island in the South Seas, in which one of the Polynesian warriors had wreaked havoc among his foes with a heavy club. Striding about the room, Melville demonstrated the feats of valor and the desperate drama of the battle. After he'd gone, Mrs. Hawthorne thought she remembered that he'd left empty-handed, and wondered, "Where is that club with which Mr. Melville was laying about him so?" Mr. Hawthorne maintained that he must have taken it with him, and indeed a search of the room revealed nothing. The next time they saw him they asked what happened to the club. It turned out that there was no club; it had simply been a figment of their imagination, conjured up by the vividness of Melville's narrative[1].

That is the power of narrative! *How* we tell our narrative can transport the audience from the location where we're telling our narrative to the location where the events took place. An expertly and impassioned telling of narrative can impact people so much, they can begin to see a club that doesn't exist! Can that be said of how you *tell* your narrative?

A large part of our narrative is based on what we say about the characters in our story. One of the most important parts in our narrative is the setting — the circumstances that surround the life and actions of our characters. The way you paint the picture of the setting allows the audience to engage deeply in the narrative, or it can repel the audience from the narrative. When the proverbial "stuff" hits the fan, what do you say about your circumstances? Do you use that as an opportunity to justify or confirm the reason why you don't dream big? After all, every time you dream big, life always happens so that you can't or don't win, right? Or do you use the opportunity to reevaluate your assumptions, goals, and plans?

When I asked my research participants what types of narratives they told about their circumstances, they overwhelmingly told a narrative that was self-enlargening. Participants chose a perspective and narrative built around growth and being steeled by adversity — they each adopted a *growth* mindset. Participants discovered that they had grit because they refused to quit; additionally, they felt as if they grew as professionals and their experience made them stronger. As painful and difficult as their circumstances were, participants focused on the capabilities that would result from their adversity. The descriptions they used for becoming stronger because of their circumstances covered a multitude of areas in their lives: relationships with others, the ability to be courageous, the ability to handle difficult times and situations, and stronger relationships with the self, to name a few. My participants exemplified the proverb that says it's better to walk than to curse the road.

How do *you* process the circumstances before, during, and after disruption? Do you blame the circumstances for your failure to launch? Do you focus your energies on the unfairness of your circumstances? If you take this posture, it's important you know that *there's no growth without personal responsibility*. Being strong doesn't *happen* to you; being strong is an *intentional* process. Body builders don't passively become strong and muscular; they intentionally combine nutrition and working out to achieve their intended results. Effective leaders aren't the result of holding a title; they're a result of intentional moves that focus on those being led. No one becomes an effective parent because they have children; effective parents are the result of carefully calculated sacrifices of time, talent, and treasure. Great things generally happen for people who are intentional and take responsibility for their part in this production called life.

I have no illusions about the circumstances that surround me and you every day. It can feel as if you're completely losing control when everything around you seems to be headed towards a cliff. Personal loss, drowning debt, betrayal, rejection, joblessness — these are hard pills to swallow. I know because I've experienced and endured every single one of them. Like most normal human beings, sitting in a Personal Loss or Joblessness course wasn't my idea of the setting for learning about grit. Experiencing betrayal and rejection definitely wasn't the way I wanted to learn gratitude. Thing is, it's not about my ideas or the ways that I prefer to learn; it's about milking the circumstances dry of every last drop. It's about maturely seeing where I am as a necessary part of my journey.

And now that I've put the image of milking in your mind, let me tell you that cows don't *give* you milk; you have to *take* it! Growing up on our farm in Lusaka, my brothers and I milked the cows at 4am and 4pm. Sure, we had workers, but my parents refused to waste an opportunity to develop character in us. Trust me when I tell you two things: first, you develop a lot of character when you're *that* close to a cow and, second, you learn that good things are earned. When I read the Bible and hear about the Israelites being led to the land of milk and honey by God Himself, I'm envious but wonder: who's going to do the milking!?

I don't know how other dairies were, but I know that our cows, even though weighed down by milk-filled udders, were not brimming with excitement at the prospect of being milked. We had to bribe them with special feed just to get them in the milking area; even so, they'd kick and scream — okay, maybe I'm exaggerating a little about screaming. My point is that at 4am and 4pm, each cow had to be milked by hand and the cows were not willing participants. Every last drop of milk we got from the cows came with hard work, cramped fingers, and the splendid joy of smelling like a cow. Your circumstances, if you change your perspective, may not be willing participants in your education. They may be weighed down with gallons of lessons that'll transform your life. There's only one person who can milk those lessons; and it's certainly not me, because I retired from milking cows at 19.

You and I have a choice every day whether we tell others a narrative of doom and gloom, or a narrative filled with hope and potential. When the narrative we tell about our circumstances sets us up for failure, we have forfeited all rights to a life well-lived. When cows don't get milked, the milk sours. For a dairy farm, that's profit lost due to laziness; for you and me, circumstances not milked simply means that we prolong the circumstances causing distress and disruption. That, alone, should be motivation for us to do everything we can to maturely draw everything we can from our circumstances.

I'd like to end this chapter and this section with a fantastic story about Frank Baum, author of *The Wonderful Wizard of Oz*. Baum's first book began when a group of children, including his own four sons, asked him to tell them a story one evening at his house in Chicago. He launched directly into a tale about a Kansas farm girl, Dorothy, and spun out her adventures. When one of the children asked him what country Dorothy had landed in, Baum looked about for inspiration. The first thing he saw was a filing cabinet, labeled O-Z. "The land of Oz!" he cried[2]. Baum's circumstances were milked for every last drop for his story; today, 119 years later, we're all still enthralled by his story. Will *you* roll your sleeves and get downright intimate with your circumstances and milk them for their treasure?

3 Tools for Your Toolbox

1. Circumstances are neutral; that is, until we attach our thoughts.
2. Life doesn't give out great things; we have to milk it.
3. What I say about my circumstances can make or break me.

PART III

Now that we've talked about a model for maturely facing the disruptions in our lives, and talked about the power of narrative, I'd like to turn to a discussion on how we can *reclaim* our narrative. Sometimes life happens, and we allow the circumstances to dictate the direction and destination of our narrative. None of us is immune from this happening. No matter how mature we are, we're human; and human nature dictates that we'll get distracted by shiny things posing as treasure. I'd like us to spend a few moments discussing a couple of tools for reclaiming our narrative. It's time for us to take back our narrative!

11. Owning Our Narrative

WHEN YOU TAKE CHARGE OF YOUR OWN NARRATIVE,
IT GIVES YOU A HANDLE ON IT.
Liz Murray

My first movie theater experience came courtesy of my brother Francis. I don't remember much, but I know it was a Klaus Kinski movie and it was a theater on Cha Cha Cha Road in downtown Lusaka. I can attempt to fill in the missing pieces, but they're unimportant. What's most important is what that experience meant to me — my older brother taking an interest in me and creating a happy experience that lives on 30-plus years later. About 10 years later, Francis took me to my first concert — a Boyz II Men concert in Johannesburg, South Africa. To Francis, these excursions were a big brother showing his little brother a good time; for me, they were defining moments of my maturing into a young man through a diverse experience provided by my big brother. I have a special bond with Francis because of these and other experiences, and his involvement has shaped me in remarkable ways.

Not long after our Boyz II Men concert, I flew to New York City from Johannesburg to begin my big dream. Perhaps it's fortuitous that we saw Boyz II Men; I went from being a boy to being a man as I crossed the Atlantic Ocean in search of the courage to pen the next chapters of my narrative. During our time together in South Africa, Francis shared his own journey from Lusaka to Johannesburg and his missteps and triumphs. I'm not sure if he realized it then, but his part in my narrative was changing from big brother to friend. No longer would he be able to directly shape my narrative; that job would fall to me — and he wanted me to write the best possible narrative. Twenty-two years after Francis and I said our goodbyes at the airport, I was able to generate some firsts for him when he came to visit us recently. It was time for his friend — and still his favorite little brother — to put his fingerprint on Francis's narrative.

I've told my clients for years that if they don't manage their schedule, someone else will. I'd like to extend the same warning to you, with a twist: *If you don't take ownership of your narrative, someone else will.* In the age of Twitter and instant communications, it's so easy for a thought or act to become part of a narrative owned by others. When others — especially those closest to us — begin to direct the movie of our lives, we no longer own our narrative. I'm not talking about the people we allow to co-create our narrative like our significant others, children, or very close friends; I'm talking about people who have too much time on their hands and work diligently to tell us what our narrative needs to be. I don't need to tell you who they are; you're thinking about them right now!

Human beings are built for community. Narratives would be meaningless if they weren't set in community. It would be like a movie showing to an empty theater — what a waste! Just because we were built for community, and our narrative thrives in the middle of community, doesn't mean that the community gets to dictate and direct our narrative. Part of living in community seems to be about learning the skill of expertly juggling between keeping people in our community happy and living out our best life. I have a newsflash for you: *It's not your job to keep people in your community happy!*

The moment we cede our happiness to someone else, we no longer own our narrative — *they* do! When our happiness is *dependent* on someone else, they can steer the ship of our emotions at will. Nothing can be more destructive than such a co-dependent relationship. Owning our narrative requires us to be resolute in ensuring that our happiness, joy, and other emotions are not influenced too easily by others. Before you think I'm nuts, give me a moment to explain further.

My wife Tabitha is my best friend. When we first met, I wasn't looking for another friend or romantic interest. Our first go at getting to know each other was unsuccessful, but we reconnected about six months later and have been inseparable ever since. Our friendship and relationship are built on a fairly simple principle: Neither of us can be the other's *whole* cake. By this I mean that neither of us can bring *everything* the other needs. I've been playing basketball with the same group of guys for over 15 years; what they bring, Tabitha can't. Tabitha's best friend brings something that I can't bring. Additionally, and perhaps most importantly, it's an unfair ask for either of us to make the other happy — that's assuming way too much control in someone's life.

My joy every day doesn't come from making my wife happy; my joy comes from making her *happier*! It's not my job to make my wife strong; my job is to make her *stronger*! If you get the logic, you can see that I show up to bring *increase* in her life; not to build. When she's happy, I make her *happier*; when she's kind, I make her *kinder*; when she's successful, I make her *more* successful. And she does the same for me. I'm happier, kinder, smarter, more patient, and so much more because of Tabitha. She came into my life to bring increase, and she does that with each passing day. By doing this for each other, we expect each other to own our happiness, our kindness, our strengths, and more — in other words, we own our narrative.

As a performance psychologist, I see so many people sign over ownership of their narratives to traffic, bullies, parents, spouses, children, grandchildren, and, dare I say, pets. So many people say they'll be happy *when*, or kind *when*, or strong *when* — the problem is that something or someone else is writing their narrative because that something or someone owns the narrative. There's a very good reason why unhappy people don't become happy when they win the lottery or make it big. A successful sports athlete or corporate athlete who was unhappy before becoming successful will remain unhappy; mostly likely, that person will become even more unhappy. Happy, kind, gentle, compassionate, or strong people generally become more of what they were before becoming successful. Waiting until you catch your big break to be happy, compassionate, strong, or any other adjective is dumb; even more, it's damaging to your narrative as it limits the impact and reach of your narrative. At some point, we have to take back the pen and write the plot, subplots, and characters in our narrative; if we don't, someone else will do it for us.

I want to own my narrative — 100%. My wife, goddaughter, close friends, and a few others will *always* have co-creating credits to my narrative; however, the bulk of the work falls on me. This life we live is too precious to leave in someone else's hands; I plan on living a *blockbuster*, and I'm not going to let someone else dictate or direct it.

You might be thinking that all of this makes me out to be a control freak; I suppose it does. If you were tasked with writing the story of the Century, wouldn't you be a control freak? If you were asked to create characters, plots, and subplots of a life well-lived, wouldn't you shape them in a way most aligned with *your* deepest values? Sure, you would! Well, with each breath, and each passing moment, you're penning the story of the Century and creating the characters, plots, and subplots of a life well-lived — it's called your *life*!

I don't know how long you've stood on the sidelines of your life, but it's time to get in the game! I'm not sure what's stopped you from cancelling the contract you used to sign your narrative away, but it's time for a breach of contract! The longer you wait, the harder it'll be to take back the pen and begin writing your narrative to fit your deepest values. It's time...

3 Tools for Your Toolbox

1. Just as easily as you gave up your narrative, you can take it back!
2. Giving up control of your narrative is giving up your life.
3. Others can contribute, but they can't be the basis of your narrative

12. Shaping Our Narrative

CREATING A RELATABLE NARRATIVE MEANS DIGGING DEEP, ASKING HARD QUESTIONS AND POTENTIALLY AIRING UNCOMFORTABLE TRUTHS.
Tobin Trevarthen

Demosthenes is generally considered the greatest orator of classical antiquity. His first attempt as a speaker came when he made a claim against his guardian, who'd defrauded him. The fortunate outcome prompted him to embark on the career of an orator. When he first took part in the public debates, his speech was so terribly delivered that the audience couldn't understand him and laughed him out of the assembly. The actor Satyrus caught up with him as he was going home discouraged; then and there, Satyrus gave him a lesson in how to deliver a speech. Demosthenes immediately took to private study for weeks at a time. To protect himself against the temptation of going out into society, he shaved one side of his head so that he'd be too embarrassed to show himself in public. He cured his stammer by speaking with pebbles in his mouth and his shortness of breath by reciting poetry while running uphill. It's through this exercise that he acquired the skill to hold an Athenian audience spellbound[1].

As I mentioned earlier, I began my career on the speaking circuit. My undergraduate work is in Speech Communication — a major now called Communication Studies. The first time I read about the great orators of classical antiquity, I was taken. In fact, it was those orators that sealed my undergraduate fate because I was a math and engineering major at the time. Demosthenes. Would you go to his lengths to not just reclaim your narrative, but to shape it? Perhaps I should ask the question differently: *What* would you be willing to do to shape your narrative in a way that is most meaningful to you? What sacrifices would you be willing to make in order to live your best life? What level of preparedness would you be willing to reach in order to use disruption to springboard you into your glorious future?

Everywhere you look, it's clear that someone is doing their very best to insert themselves into your narrative. Just about every commercial on television or the Internet is meant to give us a *craving*; they're meant to make us feel as if something is missing. So, we fill our narrative with people, places, and things that don't align with our deepest values — all in the hope that they'll scratch the itch we feel so deep within. The truth, my friend, is that people, places, and things aren't the problem; *we* are! We have to resolve to fill our narrative only with the people, places, and things that matter the most to our narrative, and put us on the path to writing an epic narrative. Remember: When we let external forces shape our narrative, we can't possibly *own* the narrative.

Disruptions come to help us stay honest. When things are hard, what is most true in us comes forth. If we've been doing the internal work to be whole and circumspect, disruptions reveal a wholesome attitude and responses that speak to a well-thought perspective. If we've been lazy and failed to do our homework, disruptions showcase just how poorly prepared we are — and the disruption will deliver a crushing blow. Shaping our narrative is about doing the hard *internal* work of asking ourselves challenging and in-your-face questions. We go beyond asking *if* something matters to us; we ask *why* it matters to us. We question our motives to make sure that we're not aligning ourselves with people, places, and things that aren't in our best interest — the best interest of our narrative.

I don't know what your spiritual beliefs are, but I have this vision that one day I'm going to be held accountable for my narrative. I'm going to be required to justify my choices, my reactions, and other parts of my narrative; I'll have to answer *the* question of my life: *Did you write a narrative that spoke to your deepest values and had the most reach and impact?* I want so desperately to be able to answer affirmatively. I want to be able to say: "Heck, yeah!" How do I make sure that I'm able to do that? By shaping my narrative; by making sure I'm very careful about the plots, subplots, and characters that are in my narrative.

I can't control most circumstances. What I can control is the plot, the subplot, and characters; by this I mean that I can control the people that come *into* my narrative and I can dictate the setting or places in my narrative. I can't control people; they'll do what they do. But I can control if they're a significant part of my narrative. Here's an example: I have a *zero*-tolerance policy for drama. There's no circumstance under which I can justify drama. By the way, my child suffering through a break-up is not drama; that's a disruption, and I'm going to be there to ease the pain. Drama is letting a relative dictate the terms of every family gathering because we don't want to hurt her feelings. I'm not interested in that. As Homey D. Clown from *In Living Color* would say: Homey don't play that!

Those kinds of people and places aren't great for my narrative. They contaminate my narrative with negativity and, frankly, foolishness. I don't have illusions of my narrative being devoid of silly drama like that; I am, however, vigilant about keeping it to bare minimum. Life's too short to be bogged down by petty drama and foolishness. My work is to *always rise* above the drama in the moment; it's also to have the courage to walk away from the people, places, and things that produce the drama.

In the previous chapter we talked about adjectives such as happy, kind, and compassionate. They are the building blocks of a life well-lived. You and I can't expect someone to come into our life and bring them into our lives. What others *can* do, though, is bring *increase*; we're happier, kinder, and more compassionate because they're in our lives. In that same light, I'd like you to think of the nouns in your life. Nouns are the people, places, and things in your life. Please be a control freak about the people, places, and things you allow into your narrative. Not all people, places, and things are good for you; that means they're not good for your narrative.

One of the things I asked my research participants was to whom and where they went during their disruption. The results showed that my participants successfully overcame their disruption and reintegrated resiliently because they didn't simply mind their Ps and Qs — they minded their adjectives and nouns. They surrounded themselves with people who would call their foolishness out while encouraging them to essentially write or rewrite a narrative that would be epic in spite of their painful disruption. In case it's not obvious, they didn't go looking for these people, places, or things when the disruption happened; they already had them, and these people, places, and things served as a lighthouse to bring them safely into port during their storm.

I've always been fascinated by lighthouses. I grew up in a landlocked country, so I never saw a lighthouse until I left Zambia. Lighthouses serve multiple purposes, including as a navigational marker. I think their most important function is that they signal that we're home. The seas of life can be treacherous, rough, and vast; lighthouses announce that, though beaten and battered, we're home — we're safe. The people, places, and things in your life should be a lighthouse. Now, because I used the word safe, I need to clarify something: finding safety in the wrong people, places, or things doesn't make for a compelling and value-driven narrative. Our goal is to have lighthouses that are true; they are unshakable, have integrity, and bring safety because they don't put up with our foolishness, immaturity, or pity parties. That's why it's so important for us to carefully ensure that all people, places, and things in our narrative align with our deepest values and hold us accountable to the truth — no matter whether we like the truth or not.

Shaping our narrative takes a great deal of *courage*. It requires us to be truthful with ourselves and give ourselves no slack for foolishness. Shaping our narrative requires *discipline*. We have to be willing to do whatever it takes — within healthy confines, of course — to make sure our narrative is compelling, epic, and reflective of our deepest values. Without courage and discipline, we can't possibly write a spellbinding narrative.

As you think about your narrative, I hope you'll filter it through the adjective and noun test. I hope you'll check to make sure that the narrative you're writing with your thoughts, words, and actions is reflective of your deepest values. I hope you'll think about how your narrative impacts others — especially those you love the most — and how it's meant to be inspirational. We can't all inspire thousands, but we can inspire one person and watch the ripple of that inspiration travel across generations and circles of influence.

That, my friend, is how powerful your narrative is; it can travel through time and space — all because you chose to write it in a *meaningful* way.

3 Tools for Your Toolbox

1. Mind your adjectives and nouns; they build your narrative.
2. Be willing to go to insane lengths for a compelling narrative.
3. Your narrative travels through time and space.

EPILOGUE

You've made it to the end of the book. Congratulations! Your narrative, however, isn't finished; no one's is until they leave the earth. Until that day, we're all obligated to use our time, talent, and treasure to write a narrative that is reflective of who we *really* are and what we genuinely value the most. Anything less is tragic and robs us all of your story...

NOTES

Chapter 2

1. Loehr, J.E. (1997). *Stress for success: The proven program for transforming stress into positive energy at work.* New York: Times Business.
2. Loehr, J.E. (1997). *Stress for success: The proven program for transforming stress into positive energy at work.* New York: Times Business.
3. Cevenini, G., Fratini, I., & Gambassi, R. (2012). A new quantitative approach to measure perceived work-related stress in Italian employees. *International Journal of Occupational Medicine and Environmental Health, 25*(4), 426-445.
4. McIntosh, D. & Horowitz, J. (2017). *Stress: The psychology of managing pressure.* New York: DK Publishing.
5. McGonigal, K. (2015). *The upside of stress: Why stress is good for you, and how to get good at it.* New York: Avery.
6. Dullat, S. & Trama, S. (2012). Yoga, meditation and soothing humor: A healthy way to handle workplace stress. *Indian Journal of Positive Psychology, 3*(4), 435-439.
7. Rani, P.B. & Yadapadithaya, P.S. (2018). *Indian Journal of Commerce & Management Studies, 9*(1), 7-12.
8. McIntosh, D. & Horowitz, J. (2017). *Stress: The psychology of managing pressure.* New York: DK Publishing.

Chapter 3

1. Fadiman, C. & Bernard, A. (2000). Bartlett's® book of anecdotes (Galen, p.224). Boston: Little, Brown and Company.
2. Castro-Solano, A. & Lupano-Perugini, M.L. (2014). The Latin-American view of positive psychology. *Journal of Behavioral, Health, & Social Sciences, 5*(2), 15-31.
3. Castro-Solano, A. & Lupano-Perugini, M.L. (2014). The Latin-American view of positive psychology. *Journal of Behavioral, Health, & Social Sciences, 5*(2), 15-31.
4. Reeve, J. (2015). *Understanding motivation and emotion.* (6th ed.). Hoboken, NJ: John Wiley & Sons.

Chapter 4

1. Tedeschi, R.G. & Calhoun, L.G. (2004). The foundations of posttraumatic growth: New considerations. *Psychological Inquiry, 15,* 93-102.
2. Shuwiekh, H., Kira, I.A., & Ashby, J.S. (2018). What are the personality and trauma dynamics that contribute to posttraumatic growth? *International Journal of Stress Management, 25*(2), 181-194.

3. Blackie, L.E.R., Roepke, A.M., Hitchcott, N., & Joseph, S. (2016). Can people experience posttraumatic growth after committing violent acts? *Journal of Peace Psychology, 22*(4), 409-412.
4. Joseph, S. (2018). After the genocide in Rwanda: Humanistic perspectives on social processes of post-conflict posttraumatic growth. *The Humanistic Psychologist.*
5. Romans 5: 3-4, New Living Translation.
6. Tedeschi, R.G., Shakespeare-Finch, J., Taku, K, & Calhoun, L.G. (2018). *Posttraumatic growth: Theory, research, and applications.* San Francisco: Routledge

Chapter 5

1. Willis, K.D. & Burnett, H.J. (2016). The power of stress: Perceived stress and its relationship with rumination, self-concept clarity, and resilience. *North American Journal of Psychology, 18,* 483-498.
2. Sharma, A. (2012). Impact of well-being on resiliency to stress. *Indian Journal of Positive Psychology, 3*(4), 440-444.
3. Kanter, R.M. (2013). Surprises are the new normal; resilience is the new skill. Retrieved June 1, 2018 from the Harvard Business Review website at https://hbr.org/2013/07/surprises-are-the-new-normal-r
4. Zolli, A. & Healy, A.M. (2013). *Resilience: Why things bounce back.* New York: Simon & Schuster Paperbacks.
5. Masten, A.S. (2001). Ordinary magic: Resilience processes in development. *American Psychologist, 56*(3), 227-238.
6. Flach, F. (1988). *Resilience: Discovering a new strength at times of stress.* New York: Fawcett Columbine.
7. McIntosh, D. & Horowitz, J. (2017). *Stress: The psychology of managing pressure.* New York: DK Publishing.

Chapter 6

1. Keye, M.D. & Pidgeon, A.M. (2013). An investigation of the relationship between resilience, mindfulness, and academic self-efficacy. *Open Journal of Social Sciences, 1*(6), 1-4.
2. John 10:10, New International Version.
3. Richardson, G.E. (2002). The metatheory of resilience and resiliency. *Journal of Clinical Psychology, 58*(3), 307-321.
4. Mukherjee, S. & Kumar, U. (2017). Psychological resilience: A conceptual review of theory and research. In Kumar, U. (Ed). *The Routledge International Handbook of Psychological Resilience* (pp. 2-11). London: Routledge.
5. Richardson, G.E. (2002). The metatheory of resilience and resiliency. *Journal of Clinical Psychology, 58*(3), 307-321.
6. Flach, F. (1988). *Resilience: Discovering a new strength at times of stress.* New York: Fawcett Columbine.

7. Keye, M.D. & Pidgeon, A.M. (2013). An investigation of the relationship between resilience, mindfulness, and academic self-efficacy. *Open Journal of Social Sciences, 1*(6), 1-4.
8. Richardson, G.E. (2002). The metatheory of resilience and resiliency. *Journal of Clinical Psychology, 58*(3), 307-321.
9. Richardson, G.E. (2002). The metatheory of resilience and resiliency. *Journal of Clinical Psychology, 58*(3), 307-321.
10. Richardson, G.E. (2002). The metatheory of resilience and resiliency. *Journal of Clinical Psychology, 58*(3), 307-321.
11. Fletcher, D. & Sarkar, M. (2013). Psychological resilience: A review and critique of definitions, concepts, and theory. *European Psychologist, 18*(1), 12-23.
12. Galli, N. & Vealey, R.S. (2008). "Bouncing back" from adversity: Athletes' experiences of resilience. *The Sport Psychologist, 22*, 316-335.
13. Richardson, G.E. (2002). The metatheory of resilience and resiliency. *Journal of Clinical Psychology, 58*(3), 307-321.
14. Mukherjee, S. & Kumar, U. (2017). Psychological resilience: A conceptual review of theory and research. In Kumar, U. (Ed). *The Routledge International Handbook of Psychological Resilience* (pp. 2-11). London: Routledge.
15. Richardson, G.E. (2002). The metatheory of resilience and resiliency. *Journal of Clinical Psychology, 58*(3), 307-321.
16. Richardson, G.E. (2002). The metatheory of resilience and resiliency. *Journal of Clinical Psychology, 58*(3), 307-321.
17. Richardson, G.E. (2002). The metatheory of resilience and resiliency. *Journal of Clinical Psychology, 58*(3), 307-321.
18. Mukherjee, S. & Kumar, U. (2017). Psychological resilience: A conceptual review of theory and research. In Kumar, U. (Ed). *The Routledge International Handbook of Psychological Resilience* (pp. 2-11). London: Routledge.
19. Richardson, G.E. (2002). The metatheory of resilience and resiliency. *Journal of Clinical Psychology, 58*(3), 307-321.
20. Richardson, G.E., Neiger, B.L., Jensen, S., & Kumpfer, K.L. (1990). The resiliency model. *Health Education, 21*(6), 33-39.

Chapter 7

1. Loehr, J.E. (2007). *The power of story: Rewrite your destiny in business and in life*. New York: Free Press.
2. Richardson, G.E., Neiger, B.L., Jensen, S., & Kumpfer, K.L. (1990). The resiliency model. *Health Education, 21*(6), 33-39.
3. Loehr, J.E. (2007). *The power of story: Rewrite your destiny in business and in life*. New York: Free Press.
4. Richardson, G.E. (2002). The metatheory of resilience and resiliency. *Journal of Clinical Psychology, 58*(3), 307-321.
5. Neenan, M. (2018). *Developing resilience: A cognitive-behavioral approach*. (2nd ed.). New York: Routledge.

6.   Hildon, Z., Smith, G., Netuveli, G., & Blane, D. (2008). Understanding adversity and resilience at older ages. *Sociology of Health & Illness, 30*(5), 726-740.
7.   Neenan, M. (2018). *Developing resilience: A cognitive-behavioral approach.* (2nd ed.). New York: Routledge.
8.   Lankford, V. (2012). My whole life is Plan B: A psychological and practical approach to resilience. *Transactional Analysis Journal, 42,* 62-70.
9.   Lankford, V. (2012). My whole life is Plan B: A psychological and practical approach to resilience. *Transactional Analysis Journal, 42,* 62-70.
10.   Fletcher, D. & Sarkar, M. (2013). Psychological resilience: A review and critique of definitions, concepts, and theory. *European Psychologist, 18*(1), 12-23.

Chapter 8

1.   BEETHOVEN (7) in Bartlett's Book of Anecdotes.
2.   Matsui, T & Taku, K (2016). A review of posttraumatic growth and help-seeking behavior in cancer survivors: Effects of distal and proximate culture. *Japanese Psychological Review, 58*(1), 142-162.
3.   Mishlei (Proverbs) 4:23, Complete Jewish Bible
4.   Proverbs 4:23, Contemporary English Version

Chapter 9

1.   FORD (4) in Bartlett's Book of Anecdotes.
2.   Beebe, S.A., Beebe, S.J., & Redmond, M.V. (2014). *Interpersonal communication: Relating to others* (7th ed.). New York: Pearson.

Chapter 10

1.   MELVILLE (1) in Bartlett's Book of Anecdotes.
2.   BAUM (2) in Bartlett's Book of Anecdotes.

Chapter 12

1.   DEMOSTHENES (1,2) in Bartlett's Book of Anecdotes.

About the Author

D r. Kozhi Sidney Makai is a "multi-hyphenate"...author, educator, social researcher, speaker, life strategist, advisor, business entrepreneur, and social entrepreneur. His sole mission is to use behavioral science to help others thrive. He is the author of award-winning social research, business and self-help books, mentor to doctoral students, speaker to small and medium-sized businesses, corporations, nonprofits, and educational institutions, advisor and coach to corporate executives, and social entrepreneur across the globe for causes from child welfare to educational programs. He resides in The Woodlands, Texas, with his wife Tabitha.

BONUS MATERIAL

Ever wondered how and why it is that storms seem to sink your boat while others' rise? If you were honest, could you say that you overcome obstacles instead of them overcoming you? Have you been discouraged by the sheer volume of things not going your way and your dreams turning into nightmares? If you responded "yes" to just one of these questions, you're not alone.

Discouragement, disappointment, and several other negative emotions hide like a cop on the highway – waiting to pull us over and give us a ticket. In *Born Beating the Odds*™, my goal is to help you see that your past trials and disappointments are merely steppingstones leading to your personal and professional growth. I remind you that you can change your pain to power and your disappointments to drive. As the title suggests, you were born beating the odds and I provide insights into raising your boat in the storm, taking back your dreams, and becoming an overcomer.

What follows is an excerpt from *Born Beating the Odds*™. Enjoy…

Introduction

I believe man can be elevated; man can become more and more endowed with divinity; and as he does he becomes more God-like in his character and capable of governing himself.[1]

Born Beating the Odds™? Yes. *Born Beating the Odds™*. My titles seem to have an interesting appeal (which makes my publicists very happy) but have very deep and significant meaning for me. Much like my previous book, there's a story behind *Born Beating the Odds™*.

The story behind this title begins in undergraduate school and spans about five years. It began in my Human Sexuality course with Dr. Johnson and my Human Development course with Dr. Cruise. The technical and psychological aspects of human growth, development, and sexuality combined with reflective thought were the potent combination that led me to say to my friend Shaun:

> Did you know that at the time of sexual intercourse, a man will generally deposit between 100 and 500 million sperm? Furthermore, do you realize that with a viability of 24 hours (and, technically, *up to* 48 hours), the *one* sperm that *wins* the mammoth "Fertilization Race" has beaten *tremendous* odds? Several hundred million to one odds, specifically...

Now, at first glance, you're probably thinking: "I thought this was supposed to be an "inspirational" book and not a dissertation on human biology and reproduction." You're absolutely right. Humor me for the next few moments, however; for it is not until you understand this "biological and reproductive" *drama* that you will gain the background behind the *title* and *spirit* of this book.

This "drama" is far from over once the *one* sperm breaks through the cell wall of the egg. If you remember from your biology or human health course, the resulting fusion of egg and sperm is called a *zygote*. The zygote, at this point, is still extremely vulnerable since "for various reasons, about one-third of all zygotes die shortly after fertilization[2]." The place at which the sperm and egg meet in the reproductive tract is often unpredictable and requires that the zygote travel some six inches for implantation (attachment to the womb)...a journey that will take between three and four *days*!

Once *you* view yourself from this perspective, it should completely change how you see yourself. I hate to sound too cliché but you *are* a miracle! Not only that; just the fact that half of you fought against and beat several hundred million competitors is testimony to your awesomeness! You're not a loser! How could you be? You went head-to-head against mighty odds – mightier than King Leonidas and 300 Spartans in the ancient Battle of Thermopylae – and crossed the finish line...*first*. You're not "nothing"! You battled for three to four days to travel six inches!

In the preface, I noted my belief in you...
...now you know *why* I believe in you. You have beaten some great odds already. My questions for you *now*, then, are:

- Why not be glamorous about it?
- Why not make beating the odds a lifestyle?
- Why not finish as spectacularly as you began?
- Why not maximize your "between conception and death" time?

Furthermore:

- What has snuffed that strong, endogenic fire to "be" that brought you into this world?
- Why have you allowed the "supposed tos" to govern who you are or become?

I'm the first to admit that I don't have the "Holy Grail" to consistently beating the odds. Like you, I have insecurities I struggle with. I have fears that sometimes deter me from fully becoming the miracle I know I am. Just as you do, I deal with difficult challenges financially, emotionally, psychologically, etc., etc., so, I'm not one to "throw stones to hide *my* hands[3]". Yet, there's something exciting about realizing that I'm *not* the person that the haters, naysayers, and pessimists think me to be.

In the pages that follow, you and I will collectively work at becoming better at beating the odds. So, get your latte, hot chocolate, or tea and buckle up. You're about to embark on a life-changing journey into the heart and mind of what it takes to consistently beat the odds. You've been warned...

Notes

1. U.S. President, Andrew Jackson
2. James W. Vander Zanden (2000). *Human Development,* Seventh Edition, p.73
3. Michael Jackson (1987). *Bad.* Epic Records

1. Pain Appreciation

You have been weighed, you have been measured, and you have been found wanting[1]

Have you ever felt that way? *Inadequate? A cut below the rest? Unable to measure up?* What emotions did this feeling evoke in you? Was it self-pity? Dejection? Did you give up? Comfort yourself with the thought that "perhaps it wasn't meant to be?" Or did you simply become angry? Did this anger turn into rage? And that rage into fury? That is, your rage was so great you could have been classified as being insane?

If any of these questions rang true for you, I believe you have the BBTO Spirit™ - the "Born Beating the Odds Spirit™". You have an *understanding* of the pain and anguish that come with rejection after rejection, put-down after put-down, hurdle after hurdle, or discouragement after discouragement. Not only do you have an *understanding* of this pain and anguish, you have a deep sense of *appreciation* for it all.

"Hold up!" you say. "Did you just say 'appreciation' for pain and anguish?" Yes, I said *appreciation*. There are two kinds of people with regard to pain and anguish: those that see it as an *inconvenience* that must be *avoided* or gotten rid of at all costs and those that see it as an *opportunity* that must be *exploited* for maximum growth. Those with the BBTO Spirit™ have an appreciation for pain and anguish because they see an "Exploitation Opportunity™." They recognize that, just like a butterfly or moth fights through a tiny hole to exit its cocoon, we, too, must fight through our perils so that when we are weighed and measured, we are *not* found wanting.

A Giraffe's Tale

In the African plains, new-born giraffes learn this lesson no more than fifteen minutes after being born[2]. When they *first* get on their feet, the mother giraffe swings her long legs and kicks the living daylights out of them! Initially, this is a sad activity to behold because we'd expect more tenderness from a mother giraffe that has been carrying it's calf for 14-15 months. Yet, this process continues until the calf learns to get up quickly. You see, in the plains, the calf's protection lies within the herd. This means that it must be able to quickly get up and keep up with the herd. Anything less and it becomes the main course for lions, leopards or hyenas.

Clearly, giraffes have mastered the art of "rolling with the punches" and learning to *appreciate* and *embrace* pain and anguish. I wonder...what is it that makes us shy away from this life-changing experience? Have we become so comfortable in our technological advancements that anything resembling effort must be automated? Or have we reached a point in our history where there's no honor in *first* sowing before we enjoy a harvest?

Appreciation?

To appreciate something is to be *thankful* for it; to have *gratitude*. According to Dictionary.com, appreciation can be defined as: *the act of estimating the qualities of things and giving them their proper value*. Wow! *Estimating...quality...value*. Without turning this into an etymological discourse, let's briefly examine these three terms: to estimate; quality; and value. To estimate is to measure or give esteem to something. Quality is simply the character or nature of something. Finally, value is the *relative* worth, merit or importance of something.

When we appreciate something or someone, we are, in essence, *determining whether the character or nature of that person or thing is worth esteeming and important*. Tying this back to pain, if we appreciate pain we are saying that we see the importance it has in our lives and we esteem it for the worth it brings to our lives. If you remember the definition of "value" above, you might note that the word "relative" is in italics. This is a sign of emphasis; it's meant to emphasize the fact that how we all value things is based on many personal factors. No two people will value something equally. Some might value their children, their work, their dreams, or their world at one level while others might value each of these at a different level – it's *relative* and *subjective*.

The funny thing about "value" is that my subjective view of it doesn't matter when set against the backdrop of reality. If I were to burn a box filled with $100,000, having *subjectively* determined that the box and the paper on which the $100 bills are printed is not of high value, would that, realistically, change the value of the $100,000? Silly question, right? No matter what I think about the value of the box and the paper on which the $100 bills are printed, the inherent value of that $100,000 is not diminished.

Kicking Against the Goad

Likewise, no matter what *your subjective* view of the value of pain in your life may be, the fact remains that there's great merit and importance in pain. Instead of "kicking against the goad[3]," you're better off waking up to the reality that pain is an essential part of life and the faster you esteem it, the faster you become more of the person you're destined to be.

A goad is a stick with a sharp point or electrically-charged point. It's used to keep oxen in line. It's never the shepherd's desire to harm his animals. It just happens that sometimes the animals don't behave as the shepherd would have them behave. When they fail to adhere to the shepherd's direction, they're poked or shocked with the goad with the underlying message, "Get in line!"

Oxen often don't get the message and can sometimes be stubborn and rebellious. When they have this stubborn and rebellious streak in them, they kick against the goad. When this happens, the shepherd must make the following message clear to the animals: *It is dangerous and it will turn out badly for you to keep kicking against the goad[4].* For the oxen, it's dangerous because the shepherd won't put up with stubbornness and rebellion for long; the oxen will become t-bone steaks at dinner...

What about you and I? What does the illustration above have to do with you and I? Everything. It's dangerous for you and I to keep kicking against the goad of reality. Offering "vain and perilous resistance[5]," the end result is often bad for us if we don't clearly recognize the role that pain has in our lives. We develop an entitlement attitude that leads our lives into an uncontrollable tailspin that can only lead to certain death.

Your "death" may not be physical but you will see your dreams die before your eyes. This will then lead to you trying to live vicariously through your children. And, for this, your children will resent you and there'll be no hope of a real relationship with them. I don't mean to be a messenger of doom but this is as real as the air you're breathing right now – you may not see it but you know it's there.

Instead of trying to avoid pain, use it as a conveyor belt to your next level of life. I've written my best poetry in pain. I've played my best basketball games in pain. I've developed my most honest relationships in pain. The challenge lies not in *overcoming* the pain; the challenge lies in *accepting* it as a *necessary* and *regular* pit stop as you grow and develop.

Notes

1. Count Adhemar in *A Knight's Tale* (2001)
2. Gary Richmond in *A View from the Zoo* (2005)
3. Acts 9:5. The Amplified Bible
4. *Ibid*
5. *Ibid*

Share

DISRUPTED!

with Others.

Join us in our Vision to Help Students, Parents, and Organizations Make Resiliency a Core Value

Visit the link below for more:

www.KozhiMakai.com/Books

BORN
Beating the Odds™

DR. KOZHI SIDNEY MAKAI

Puzzle Pieces
Fostering Sustainable Partnerships

Dr. Kozhi Sidney Makai

Foreword by Dr. Steven Beebe,
Regents' and University Distinguished Professor of Communication

Our "I Dos" Were...

Different

Dr. Kozhi Sidney Makai

Made in USA - North Chelmsford, MA
1073881_9780979989124
04.08.2020 1837